HISTORY & GEOGRAPHY 1010

Ancient Times to the 21st Century

LIFEPAC Test is located in the center of the booklet. Please remove before starting the unit.

Authors:
Dorothea M. Denney, M.Ed.
Richard Morse

Editor-in-Chief:
Richard W. Wheeler, M.A.Ed.

Editor:
Richard R. Andersen, M.A.

Consulting Editor:
Rudolph Moore, Ph.D.

Revision Editor:
Alan Christopherson, M.S.

MEDIA CREDITS:
8: © Tarbod, iStock, Thinkstock; **17:** © Rafael Laguillo, Hemera, Thinkstock; **19:** © Georgios Kollidas, iStock, Thinkstock; **23:** © Photos.com, Thinkstock; **32:** © Brandon Bourdages, iStock, Thinkstock; **36:** © Elenaphoto21, iStock, Thinkstock; **41:** © TonyBaggett, iStock, Thinkstock; **44:** © Hannah-Mac, iStock, Thinkstock; **55:** © Georgios Art, iStock, Thinkstock; **57:** © runamock, iStock, Thinkstock; **58:** © Library of Congress, cph 3c10385; **63:** © CPhoM Robert F Sargent; ARC Identifier 195515; **64:** © bwzenith, iStock, Thinkstock.

Alpha Omega
PUBLICATIONS

**804 N. 2nd Ave. E.
Rock Rapids, IA 51246-1759**

Ancient Times to the 21st Century

Introduction

In the previous nine LIFEPACs you have studied the history of the world from very ancient civilizations to modern times. You will now review what you have learned. You will look once more at those ancient civilizations. You will reacquaint yourself with the Middle Ages and the Renaissance. You will see how each of these periods contributed to the modern world in which you live.

Objectives

Read these objectives. The objectives tell you what you will be able to do when you have successfully completed this LIFEPAC®. When you have finished this LIFEPAC, you should be able to:

1. List the most important ancient civilizations.
2. Explain how ancient societies governed themselves.
3. Identify the leaders of the ancient civilizations and their accomplishments.
4. Describe the cultures of the various societies.
5. Explain feudalism.
6. Show the importance of the church in the Middle Ages.
7. Point out the differences between the Middle Ages and the Renaissance.
8. Describe the politics in the major European countries during the Renaissance.
9. List the highlights of Renaissance arts and sciences.
10. Explain the Reformation.
11. Show how religious conflicts led to wars.
12. Define *absolutism*.
13. Show the development of the strongest nations in Europe.
14. Define mercantilism.
15. Trace the travels of European explorers and their claims in the New World.
16. Describe the great revolutions that helped to produce the modern world.
17. Describe the political and military career of Napoleon I.
18. List the important early inventions of the Industrial Revolution.
19. Describe the events leading to and during World War I.
20. Describe the events leading to and during World War II.
21. Outline the structure of the United Nations.
22. Discuss the important political areas in the modern world.
23. List the major international organizations today.

Survey the LIFEPAC. Ask yourself some questions about this study and write your questions here.

_____

_____

_____

_____

_____

_____

_____

_____

_____

_____

_____

_____

_____

_____

_____

_____

_____

_____

1. ANCIENT CIVILIZATIONS AND MEDIEVAL TIMES

The first section of the review will deal with the world prior to 1500. It will recall the ancient civilizations, remind you of their ending, and discuss their contributions to the world. By 1500 the nations of Western Europe were stable enough to begin searching for places to establish colonies. Spain led the way but did not handle her colonies wisely. England and France followed, and England gained the most. Out of these activities, the modern world finally began to develop.

Section Objectives

Review these objectives. When you have completed this section, you should be able to:

1. List the most important ancient civilizations.
2. Explain how ancient societies governed themselves.
3. Identify the leaders of the ancient civilizations and their accomplishments.
4. Describe the cultures of the various societies.
5. Explain feudalism.
6. Show the importance of the church in the Middle Ages.

Vocabulary

Study these words to enhance your learning success in this section.

assimilation	diocese	Ides of March	Nicene Creed
scriptorium	see	triumvirate	vernacular

Note: *All vocabulary words in this LIFEPAC appear in* **boldface** *print the first time they are used. If you are not sure of the meaning when you are reading, study the definitions given.*

HEBREWS

The Old Testament of the Bible, the gift of God through the Hebrews to the people of the world, records the most ancient of ancient times. In the opening lines, it states (Genesis 1:1) "In the beginning God created the heaven and the earth." No time existed before the beginning.

The Hebrews were the descendants of Abraham, who settled in Canaan. From Canaan, Abraham's grandson Jacob moved his family to Egypt to be reunited with his son Joseph and to provide his family with sustenance during a famine. Generations later, Moses led them back to Canaan, the Promised Land. The area that was Canaan was approximately that of Israel today.

During this time many Hebrews did not remain true to God. They fought among themselves and were attacked by outsiders. They finally saw their Holy City, Jerusalem, destroyed by the Babylonians and many of their people carried off as captives to Babylon.

In Babylon they had to choose whether to spend their time in mourning or to make captivity meaningful. They chose the latter and spent much of the next seventy years creating the framework of the Old Testament and solidifying their beliefs.

Many Jews never returned to Jerusalem. The Diaspora, which is the name given to the scattering of the Hebrews all over the world, took place. When Jesus Christ the Savior was born in Bethlehem as promised, most Jews refused to accept Him. Their descendants are still waiting for a Messiah.

Christian belief accepts the Trinity and acknowledges Christ as (I John 2:1 and 2) "...an advocate with the Father...the propitiation for our sins..." With this knowledge of God and his acceptance of the Trinity, the Christian is prepared to carry on his struggle with Satan which is his heritage from Adam and Eve. Since he believes in this manner, he must accept God's presence in the making of history.

Complete the following sentences.

1.1 The gift of God through the Hebrews to the whole world was the _____ .

1.2 Canaan was called the _____ .

1.3 The Hebrews solidified their beliefs while in _____ .

1.4 The Hebrews were the descendants of _____ .

1.5 The scattering of the Hebrew people all over the world was called the _____ .

EGYPTIANS

The land along the Nile River had the requirements for settlement: warm climate, water supply, protective mountains, and a long coastline.

Egypt, the oldest of the early civilizations, developed a calendar, a system of irrigation, written communication, and local government before it was classified as a civilization.

The first central government was formed by the uniting of Egypt's upper and lower kingdoms under King Menes in 3400 B.C. From his capital at Memphis, he ruled with a strong hand and was able to keep the two kingdoms together and start a dynasty. Later the Pharaohs, as they came to be known, were considered divine, and their words were never questioned.

Once cities were established and the government became stable, Egypt began to trade among cities up and down the Nile. Finally, it started to trade with other countries around the eastern end of the Mediterranean Sea.

The government was not always strong enough to keep out invaders. Over the centuries, Egypt was conquered several times. One group of invaders, the Hyksos in the sixteenth century B.C., brought horses and chariots with them. The horses and chariots proved very valuable to the Egyptians, who used them to attack and conquer others.

Egypt built an empire and proceeded to set up trade routes with other countries. Surplus wheat and other grains were traded for products in the Mediterranean area. Egypt was able to buy the lumber and tin it needed as well as many other products. The Phoenicians brought tin all the way from England to Egypt, and Egyptian artisans mixed copper and tin to make bronze for decoration and weapons. Scribes kept records of trade transactions as Egyptians learned the importance of records for government and trade.

Answer true or false.

1.6 _____ Egypt was settled on land along the Nile River.

1.7 _____ King Menes ruled Egypt from his capital at Hyksos.

1.8 _____ The Egyptians imported tin that came from England.

1.9 _____ Business records were kept by scribes.

1.10 _____ Egypt was such a powerful nation it was never invaded.

Complete the following sentences.

1.11 Bronze is made by mixing a. _____ and b. _____ .

1.12 The Hyksos brought the a. _____ and b. _____ to Egypt.

1.13 Four developments of the Egyptian civilization were these:

a. _____ , b. _____ ,

c. _____ , and d. _____ .

1.14 Egyptian leaders considered divine were called _____ .

| Babylon

BABYLONIANS

Between the Tigris and Euphrates rivers at the eastern end of the Fertile Crescent is located the land whose name, *Mesopotamia*, means *the land between two rivers*. Here on the plains of Shinar several groups settled. They never became true civilizations, although some of them did build empires, because they never developed beyond a city-state organization.

One of these groups was the Babylonians. Their capital city of Babylon was beautiful, and it lasted nearly two thousand years. It was in Babylon that one of the emperors, Hammurabi codified the laws of Babylonia. Hammurabi was able to unite the Babylonians, but after his death his empire disintegrated.

Most of the Babylonians remained agricultural, but they did trade with the existing civilizations. A few craftsmen made articles to sell, but most of their sales were of food grains. Babylonians used clay for building, since stone was not available. Brick remains have been located by archaeologists.

 Answer true or false.

1.15 _____ No remains of the Babylonians have ever been found.

1.16 _____ Hammurabi, emperor of Babylonia, codified the laws of his country.

CHINESE

The earliest civilization in the Far East was that of China. The Yellow and Yangtze rivers provided water. The Yellow River often flooded causing disaster for the people. Crops could not be planted, and starvation followed. Mass migrations of Chinese took place because of this condition. Northern China was settled before southern China, but the people in the south began cultivation of the Chinese staple, rice.

China had a difficult time uniting. Its feudal stage was a period of war and invasion, as it would be much later in Europe. Finally, China became one nation in the fourth century before Christ.

China is protected by mountains and the sea, but to the north are plains from which invaders came. The Huns, a fierce and warlike tribe, inhabited the area. To protect themselves from the Huns, the Chinese built the Great Wall of China about five hundred B.C. Over the years the wall began to crumble, and in the thirteenth century Genghis Khan, who had united several of the nomadic tribes north of the wall, attacked and conquered the northern Chinese. These Mongols, as they were called, swept across Asia into Russia. Genghis Khan left his empire to his grandson, Kublai Khan, who was successful in reuniting northern and southern China. It was during this time that Marco Polo came from Italy to visit China.

Under the Sung rule China reached new heights of production and trade. After the crusades, demand from Europe for Chinese products became very great. At the same time, trade routes overland became costly and dangerous. Europeans began to look for a way to reach the Far East by sailing west.

Over its history, China was divided into two classes of people, the very rich and the very poor. The poor for the most part were peasants who lived off the land. They paid high taxes to support their rulers.

Answer true or false.

1.17 _____ The Great Wall of China was built after the birth of Christ.

1.18 _____ Mesopotamia means "land between two rivers."

1.19 _____ Flooding on the Yangtze River caused great hardship for the early Chinese.

1.20 _____ Genghis Khan was the leader of the northern Chinese.

1.21 _____ After the crusades, Chinese demand for European products became very great.

Complete this writing assignment.

1.22 Research Marco Polo's visit to China and prepare a paper of approximately one hundred words telling about what he saw. Have your teacher check your paper.

TEACHER CHECK _____ _____
initials   date

GREEKS

Much of Greek civilization had its origins in the culture of Crete. The Cretans had developed a high degree of civilization before they were forced to leave their island because a fire destroyed all that they had built. The Cretans resettled in Mycenae and began trading with the Aegean city-states and Egypt. Later they attacked and destroyed the ancient city of Troy in Asia Minor. Homer, the blind Greek poet, wrote about this war and its aftermath in the *Iliad* and the *Odyssey*. The Mycenaeans were attacked and conquered in the twelfth century before Christ and with their conquerors were the forerunners of the Greek people.

Because of poor soil, early Greek city-states had to buy food from outside their borders. In exchange they sold bronze weapons and other items. This trade led to the founding of Greek colonies around the shores of the Mediterranean. Athens, almost from its beginning, was chief among the Greek city-states. The first democratic practices in government appeared in Athens. A council of 500 was made up of representatives of the people. Debates were held openly before any law was enacted.

Before its democracy was thoroughly established, Athens was attacked by Persia, which was attempting to build a Mediterranean empire. Athens sought the aid of another city-state, and together they drove the Persians from Greek territory permanently. The Athenian civilization reached its peak under Pericles after the Persians were routed. Athenian culture flourished. Trade was good, and Athens became wealthy. Democracy developed further but was never complete because only male, native born citizens could participate.

After the Age of Pericles, Greece declined. Athens and Sparta engaged in the Peloponnesian War in which Athens was defeated. Unable to defend themselves, the Greeks fell victim to Philip of Macedonia whose kingdom was to the north. His son, Alexander the Great, spread the Greek Empire and culture over the Middle East. As Greek culture mingled with the cultures of the conquered peoples, the so-called Hellenistic culture developed.

Alexander swept as far east as India. He attempted to unite the area, but was not successful. Probably his worst mistake was his failure to provide for a successor to rule after his death. The empire went into a period of decline, and the Greeks began to give way to the next civilization, Rome.

Answer the following questions.

1.23 Why were the ancient Greek city-states forced to trade outside their borders?

_____

_____

1.24 Who was Homer? _____

_____

1.25 Where did much of Greek civilization have its origins? _____

1.26 What was one of Alexander the Great's most serious mistakes? _____

_____

1.27 Who fought in the Peloponnesian War? a. _____ and b. _____ .

ROMANS

The story of Rome began with the defeat of the Etruscans for control of the city-states that had grown up around the mouth of the Tiber River. Rome was not located on the seacoast since no natural harbor indented the Italian coastline there.

During the early years, Rome followed the practice of the Etruscans and ruled with a king who took advice from a senate made up of the people from the upper classes. When dissatisfaction arose among the lower classes, the plebeians, Rome became a republic and allowed tribunes or representatives of the people to be elected and to advise. Rome was on its way to becoming a democracy. Rome took possession of the Italian peninsula either by driving out the people who already lived there or by taking them over. This takeover included the Greeks. As it established supremacy over the peninsula, Rome made the conquered people feel as if they were part of Rome by granting them Roman citizenship. At the same time, Rome assured itself of a large army when it was needed.

Rome became involved in the Punic Wars with Phoenicia over the city of Carthage in North Africa. Carthage was a Phoenician colony, and Phoenicia interfered with Roman trade in the Mediterranean. Three wars were fought over a period of more than a hundred years until Rome devastated Carthage and sold its people into slavery. Shortly afterward, the city of Corinth in Greece met almost the same fate.

Rome began to hire mercenaries to fight battles of expansion, but ensuing chaos destroyed the political gains the plebeians had made. Two men came to their support, the Gracchi brothers who were members of the senate and of the upper class. They failed to help the poor, and the result was civil war. The senators fled for their lives; and Caesar, Pompey, and Crassus tried to form a **triumvirate** to rule Rome. Crassus and Pompey, for different reasons, left the triumvirate and Caesar was left to rule alone. Fearing that he would start a line of dictators, the senators decided to get rid of Caesar, and accordingly on the **Ides of March**, 44 B.C., they stabbed him to death in the senate chambers. No one wanted to succeed Caesar although Octavian, Caesar's nephew, was his heir. Trouble over who should rule ended when Mark Antony and Octavian decided to rule together. This arrangement lasted for about ten years when Octavian was told that Antony together with Cleopatra, queen of Egypt, would try to seize control. A battle followed at Actium where Antony and Cleopatra were defeated in 31 B.C. Antony and Cleopatra committed suicide, and Egypt became a Roman province. Octavian was granted the title Augustus by the senate and went on to rule alone.

During his short term in office, Caesar had begun reforms. Octavian, later called Augustus, continued these reforms. He gave food to the poor and provided entertainment for them. Caesar had decided that all conquered people should be given Roman citizenship with all the privileges that went with it. He also made reforms in the tax system, which Augustus continued.

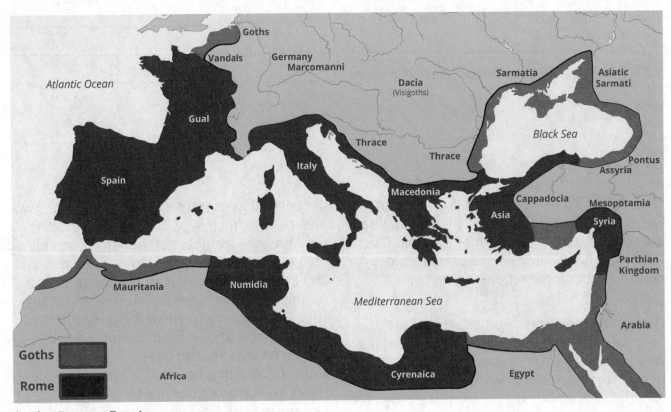

| The Roman Empire

Augustus was now ruler over a large empire, and his reign began with what would later be called the Roman Peace or as the Romans called it, *Pax Romano*. Peace allowed time and money for other activities. New trade was established with the provinces, and the empire became almost self-sufficient. North Africa furnished grain for most of the empire's bread. Roads, bridges, public buildings, and aqueducts were built. Travel became easier within the empire, and roads were filled with carts and people. Christ was born during the reign of Augustus in the town of Bethlehem in one of the Roman provinces.

After the death of Augustus peace continued: but inferior rulers outnumbered good ones. Rome went into decline. No longer able to keep invaders out, Rome found its borders under constant attack by Germanic tribes. The army was increased in size, but the cost was high. As more soldiers were needed, the cost to the people impoverished them; and inflation eroded the value of the money. Government was not only inefficient but corrupt. Civil disorder was almost constant. Emperors Diocletian and Constantine tried to solve these problems. Diocletian thought the empire was too large for one man to rule; therefore, he divided it into the Eastern and Western empires. Constantine reunited them and moved the capital to Constantinople, but even this plan to strengthen the empire failed. It was divided again after Constantine died, and from that point on the Western half declined. It was overrun by the Ostrogoths in A.D. 476, and a Germanic emperor named Odoacer took the throne. The Eastern half lived on for a thousand years and finally succumbed to the Ottoman Turks when they came into power in southwest Asia.

Complete the following sentences.

1.28 The plebeians were the _____ classes of Rome.

1.29 After defeating Antony and Cleopatra, Octavian was granted the title of _____ by the Roman senate.

1.30 To make conquered peoples feel like Romans, Rome gave them Roman _____ .

1.31 The Roman leader stabbed to death on the Ides of March, 44 B.C., was _____ _____ .

1.32 The Roman Empire was divided into Eastern and Western empires by the emperor _____ .

1.33 *Pax Romano* means _____ .

1.34 When Christ was born during the reign of Augustus, Bethlehem was a town in one of the Roman _____ .

1.35 The story of Rome began with the defeat of the _____ .

Answer this question.

1.36 Why did the Roman Empire in the west go into decline?

_____

_____

_____

_____

ANCIENT CULTURES

All of the ancient civilizations, with the exception of the Hebrews, were polytheistic; that is, they worshiped many gods. Their gods were similar in nature, and the presence of one overruling god was evident. Most civilizations developed a religion for the home that was based on nature. Several also added mysterious religious practices. The Far Eastern cultures adopted religions based on the thoughts of great men of the time, such as Confucius and Buddha. The Chinese added ancestor worship, which does not appear to have developed anywhere in the West. Among the ancient civilizations, Egypt was the only one to have a ruler who was considered to be divine.

Most ancient cultures believed in education for boys, but only Babylon made an effort to educate their daughters. The fact that all ancient cultures were interested in education indicates that they must have made a connection between success and learning. That China encouraged education more than other ancient societies was shown by the fact that government jobs were based on civil service examinations, for which a strong educational background was required.

Each society had a small, rich upper class and a large mass of lower-class poor. Middle classes were significantly smaller, but the middle class was making its beginning among people engaged in trade, business, and industry. In no case did the middle class become large enough to be a political force.

All of the civilizations traded with the other parts of the known world, and the upper classes enjoyed the products brought in. The lower class had little money or opportunity to advance. Trading nations also developed a system of bookkeeping and keeping records.

Most societies remained agricultural, with few large centers of trade. The cities had opportunities that the countryside did not: the theaters of Greece, for example, or the Circus Maximus in Rome. The lower classes in the cities apparently did get the chance to attend these public entertainments.

Most civilizations developed a written language, but Eastern languages were far different from those in the West where Rome was so long in control. Latin was the source of many languages that are still spoken today. Some written languages, like Chinese, were very complicated.

 Answer true or false.

1.37 _____ The ancient Chinese were very primitive and had no organized way to teach formal education.

1.38 _____ The religion of most ancient civilizations was polytheistic, which meant they worshiped many gods.

1.39 _____ The middle class in ancient cultures was the largest group in most countries.

1.40 _____ Confucius and Buddha both contributed to religious thought in the Far East.

1.41 _____ Most ancient societies believed in education for boys, but only Egypt made an attempt to educate girls.

1.42 _____ Latin, the language of the Roman Empire, was the source of many languages that are still spoken today.

MEDIEVAL TIMES: INVASIONS

The Middle Ages, as they are called, began with the fall of Rome and lasted approximately five hundred years. Not the Dark Ages historians once thought them to be, they still were far from the best of times. The Late Middle Ages were a time of consolidation and beginnings.

From the fall of the Roman Empire until the Middle Ages, waves of invaders swept into Western Europe. Germanic tribes moved across the continent by land, while Vikings arrived in England by sea. A major cause of these invasions was the breakup of the Roman Empire and the withdrawal of Roman soldiers from the outlying territories. Mass migrations of people seeking new lands followed. A great deal of assimilation between previous cultures and their invaders followed, and new cultures emerged.

Huns. Only once did the Romans and the Germanic tribes unite to stop an invasion. The Huns, cruel and destructive, were a common enemy. Combined armies halted the Huns and drove them back into Asia.

Vikings and Normans. England was attacked time and again by Vikings from what is now Scandinavia. Finally in the tenth century, Alfred, the Saxon king of Wessex, united Southern England against the Danes. After his death, the Danes invaded again and put a Danish king, Canute, on the throne. Before the end of the eleventh century, England was conquered by William of Normandy, a kingdom in Northern France. He seized the English throne in 1066 and unified the country.

Franks. The Franks settled in the area that today is roughly equivalent to France. King Charlemagne (Charles the Great) built an empire that stretched from the Atlantic to the Balkans and included Italy. It contained a large part of the area that once belonged to Rome. Before Charlemagne came to the throne,

his grandfather stopped the invasion of the Moors at Tours in 732. If it had not been for the defeat of the Moors, it is likely all of Europe today would be Muslim rather than Christian. By donating lands to the pope, Charlemagne's father made the church a landowner with political power as well as religious power.

In 800, the pope crowned Charlemagne emperor. Many people questioned the wisdom of this move because it seemed to suggest that the pope had power over secular rulers. Rulers and nobles believed strongly that he did not.

After Charlemagne's death, quarreling and poor leadership brought an end to the empire that he had so carefully put together. Norman invaders moved against the Franks and took from them a large area in Northwestern France. They named this area Normandy, and it was from there that William the Conqueror invaded England and took over the English throne. Thus England became a landowner in France for the next six hundred years. This arrangement led to many wars.

Others. The Vandals took over the Iberian peninsula (Spain) but were driven out by the Visigoths. The Visigoths then moved into North Africa. The Moors overran them both and forced the Muslim religion upon them.

The Muslim faith spread through the Middle East in the seventh century. One of its beliefs was that it should spread the faith by the sword. Consequently, in the eighth century, the Muslims set out to conquer the world. They swept across northern Africa and entered Europe through what is today Southern Spain. Several times during the next six hundred years, they were defeated in Spain until they remained only in Granada. King Ferdinand and Queen Isabella expelled the last of them in 1492.

Complete these sentences.

1.43 In the year A.D. 800 the pope crowned Charlemagne emperor of the land we now call

_____ .

1.44 England was attacked time and again by invaders from Scandinavia called _____ .

1.45 A major cause of the invasions that swept Western Europe before the Middle Ages was the

_____ .

1.46 Spain is located on the _____ peninsula.

1.47 The Romans and the Germanic tribes combined to defeat the _____ .

Match these items.

1.48 _____ Canute

1.49 _____ Charlemagne

1.50 _____ Ferdinand and Isabella

1.51 _____ Alfred

1.52 _____ William the Conqueror

a. conquered England in 1066

b. destroyed the Vandals

c. emperor in France

d. Danish king of England

e. united Southern England

f. drove the Moors from Spain

MEDIEVAL TIMES: FEUDALISM

In the Middle Ages the dominant social, economic, and political force was the feudal system. This system determined the course of men's lives for hundreds of years.

Causes. Lack of strong government and leadership of kings in the Middle Ages led to strong local governments under powerful nobles. These conditions led to the rise of feudalism, which was basically the same wherever it appeared in Europe. It was based on the holding of land.

Structure. In the feudal system the king, who owned all land, granted portions to nobles, church leaders, and others in positions of authority. In return, he received their promise of support with troops, money, and equipment in time of war. Those who received land had only the right to use it. They did not own it; it belonged to the king. Thus they became *vassals* of the king.

The relationship between the king and the nobles who received land from him was only the beginning of the feudal structure. Nobles granted smaller parcels of land, called *fiefs*, to lesser nobles in exchange for a loyalty oath similar to the one they had given the king. This granting of lands to lesser nobles was known as *subinfeudation*.

Lesser nobles could, in turn, grant very small parcels of land to *knights* in exchange for yet another oath of loyalty. Thus, the noble was the vassal of the king, the lesser noble was the

| Chateau de Montpoupon, France

vassal of the noble, and the knight was the vassal of the lesser noble. At every step in the feudal structure, the vassals expected to be protected in those dangerous times by those on the step above them.

The feudal system dealt only with the upper classes. Feudalism was the main system of government in medieval Europe from the tenth century on, but it was not equally strong in all parts of Europe. France was the center of early feudal society. England did not accept feudalism until it was imposed by William the Conqueror after 1066. The Germanic and Italian kingdoms used feudalism and the feudal system to a lesser degree.

Manorialism. As feudalism was the structure of the upper classes, manorialism imposed a system on the lower classes, the peasants. It defined their relationship to the nobility in the person of the Lord of the manor. The peasants for a price could live and work on a manor.

The medieval manor consisted of a manor house, a main dwelling where the lord of the manor lived; houses for peasants; a priest's house; and a church. There were mills, barns, and stables as well. Manors were well fortified against attack, and they were self-sufficient. There were few cities and towns where goods could be bought; consequently, manors had to supply their own needs.

Peasants made up most of the medieval citizenry. They had no place in the feudal system. Their function in the manorial system was to work the land, from which most of them could never escape.

Answer these questions.

1.53 What was the dominant social, economic, and political system in the Middle Ages?

_____

1.54 Under the feudal system, who owned all of the land? _____

1.55 What was a fief? _____

1.56 Who made up the large majority of medieval citizenry? _____

1.57 What would a noble who received land from the king be expected to give in return?

_____

1.58 Who imposed feudalism on England after 1066? _____

MEDIEVAL CULTURE

Although the Middle Ages have been referred to by scholars as the "Dark Ages," the times continued to produce fine examples of man's creativity. Education, too, had a place, although it was not as readily available to all segments of society as it is today.

Education. The social conditions of the twelfth and thirteenth centuries opened the way for learning. Towns were growing, the wealthy merchant class was expanding, the power of the church was enormous, and contacts were being made through trade with other cultures. Educated people were needed to fill important positions.

Learning guilds were formed. Loosely formed guilds were called *universities*, although they had no formal courses and no buildings. Later, the first formal universities were established in Bologna (1158), Paris (around 1200), and in Oxford and Cambridge in England in the late twelfth and early thirteenth centuries. Courses taught at these universities were divided into two areas: (1) the *trivium*—Latin grammar, logic, and rhetoric—and (2) the *quadrivium*—arithmetic, music, geometry, and astronomy. Science and mathematics were advanced primarily by Greek and Arab works brought into Europe at various times.

Literature and art. Advances in education and the growth of towns led to new interest in literature and the arts. Much of the literature, drama, music, art, and architecture centered around the Catholic Church.

Literature was often sung. *Minstrels* and *troubadours* traveled from town to town and manor to manor to sing their songs of fair ladies, deeds of knightly valor, and love. Social comment in written literature grew with the rise of towns. Long poems, such as *The Parliament of Three Ages* and *The Vision of Piers Plowman*, pointed out the corruption and dishonesty in government and the clergy, and the oppression of the poor. The Robin Hood legend developed at this time because it pictured the poor being championed in their cause against the rich and powerful.

Two of the most important literary men of the Middle Ages were Dante (1265-1321) and Chaucer. Alighieri Dante was an Italian poet and philosopher. His most famous work, *The Divine Comedy*, an epic journey through hell, reflects man's struggle for salvation. Dante is often hailed as the father of Italian literature because he chose to write in his native dialect rather than in Latin.

Geoffrey Chaucer (1340-1400) wrote the famous *Canterbury Tales*, a collection of medieval tales told by pilgrims on their way to Canterbury Cathedral, an English shrine. The tales represent most types of literature being written or sung in the fourteenth century.

Early medieval drama began in the church and gradually moved outside to the courtyard. Most plays dealt with Biblical or religious themes. Plays were performed in groups called *cycles*. These cycles covered the history of salvation from the Creation to Christ's Resurrection and the Last Judgment. On religious festival days these plays were performed on wagons, which stopped at designated places in the town, presented their plays, and then moved on.

Most medieval music was composed for the church and was sung in Latin. Plain song or chant was written with simple notation above each syllable. Later a more complicated music called *polyphony*, which wove several melodies together, was introduced. Popular music was sung in the **vernacular** and included the songs of troubadours and ancient ballads.

Medieval architecture was also centered in the church, which was the hub of community activity. Early medieval architecture was *Romanesque*. The late twelfth century saw the rise of the *Gothic* style of architecture. The Gothic style used high, pointed arches, walls filled with windows, and soaring effects. Carvings and statues filled the cathedrals inside and out.

| Geoffrey Chaucer

Write the letter for the correct answer on each line.

1.59 Geoffrey Chaucer wrote _____ .
   a. *The Divine Comedy*
   b. *The Vision of Piers Plowman*
   c. *The Canterbury Tales*
   d. *The Parliament of Three Ages*

1.60 Loosely formed learning guilds in the Middle Ages were called _____ .
   a. quadriviums
   b. manors
   c. troubadours
   d. universities

1.61 Most of medieval music was composed for the church and sung in _____ .
   a. Latin
   b. unison
   c. vernacular
   d. prose

1.62 Medieval plays performed in groups were called _____ .
   a. pageants
   b. cycles
   c. festivals
   d. wagon plays

1.63 The center of medieval life was the _____ .
   a. lord of the manor
   b. architecture
   c. church
   d. vernacular

1.64 The medieval legend that pictured the poor being championed by a hero who fought for them against the rich was that of _____ .
   a. Robin Hood
   b. Piers Plowman
   c. Saint Nicholas
   d. Geoffrey Chaucer

THE MEDIEVAL CHURCH

The story of the Middle Ages is not complete unless the activities of its most powerful unifying institution, the Roman Catholic Church, are described. The church made its power felt among monarchs, nobles, and peasants alike. They all feared it and followed its laws and rituals. Nevertheless, trouble sometimes erupted.

Influence. By the beginning of the Middle Ages, the doctrines of the church were clearly defined by the **Nicene Creed**. The church was organized into **dioceses** and **sees** headed by clergy and bishops. In the major population centers archbishops were in charge. Rome was already the acknowledged leader, and the title of pope had been bestowed upon its bishop. Persecution of Christians was a thing of the past, and monasteries had been established.

No question was ever raised about how to worship or what to believe during the Middle Ages. The Catholic Church was God's representative and dictated to people on almost every matter. People lived out their lives without questioning what was told them.

The church was the center of people's lives. They attended mass, received the sacraments, paid their church taxes, and lived in the shadow of the church all their lives. If they did not, they would be punished. If they became heretics, they knew that the Inquisition was ready to seek them out and to punish them.

The church handed down directives and laws of society to obey. *The Peace of God* and the *Truce of God* forbade fighting on certain days, made looting churches and monasteries a crime, made the monasteries havens of safety where no attack was permitted, and provided for punishment if the rules were broken. The church grew wealthy through gifts, inheritances, rents, taxes, and fees.

Nicene Creed

I believe in one God, the Father Almighty, maker of heaven and earth, and of all things visible and invisible;

And in one Lord Jesus Christ, the only begotten Son of God, begotten of his Father before all worlds, God of God, Light of Light, very God of very God, begotten, not made, being of one substance with the Father; by whom all things were made; who for us men and for our salvation came down from heaven, and was incarnate by the Holy Ghost of the Virgin Mary, and was made man; and was crucified also for us under Pontius Pilate; he suffered and was buried; and the third day he rose again according to the Scriptures, and ascended into heaven, and sitteth on the right hand of the Father; and he shall come again, with glory, to judge both the quick and the dead; whose kingdom shall have no end.

And I believe in the Holy Ghost the Lord, and Giver of Live, who proceedeth from the Father [and the Son]; who with the Father and the Son together is worshipped and glorified; who spake by the Prophets. And I believe one holy Catholic and Apostolic Church; I acknowledge one baptism for the remission of sins; and I look for the resurrection of the dead, and the life of the world to come. AMEN.

Struggles. At times the church created and destroyed kings. Its position was that a monarch or emperor stayed on the throne only so long as the church wanted him there. Royalty, of course, thought differently. Most of these arguments were settled by war or threat of war. If the monarch was stronger, he won. If the pope was stronger, he prevailed.

Most of the struggles over the appointment of emperors and kings took place in the Holy Roman Empire. One notable argument with King John of England, however, ended with John handing over England as a fief to the pope. Another incident in France over the appointment of a French king led to the Avignon Captivity when the papacy was moved to France and French popes were chosen for nearly one hundred years.

Other disputes arose, such as who was to get a bishop's land when he died. Both church and monarch claimed it. Bishops were appointed to their sees by the pope, but often a monarch in need of aid with the running of his government would grant a fief to a bishop in return for his help. This struggle went on for years. Finally a compromise was arranged in which the pope appointed the bishop and took care of all matters concerning the church, and the government dealt with land and all things concerning the bishop's relationship with the king.

The church was a unifying force in Western Europe, but in Germany and Italy unification was delayed because of its presence. After Otto I, a few strong emperors became leaders of the Holy Roman Empire. Germany eventually broke up into many small states, however, with each governing itself. These states backed the emperor in his fights with the popes, and they were desirous that the Holy Roman Empire hold Italian land. Italy was divided because the Holy Roman Empire held part of its northern land and the papal lands split the rest of the country in two. Germany and Italy were not unified until the nineteenth century, and both became a source of trouble to the world because they did not unite when the rest of Europe did.

Answer true or false.

1.65 _____ The church was the most powerful unifying institution in the Middle Ages.

1.66 _____ The Peace of God and the Truce of God forbade all warfare in the Middle Ages.

1.67 _____ During the period of the Avignon Captivity, the papacy was moved from Rome to France.

1.68 _____ Until the nineteenth century, Germany and Italy were the only fully unified nations in Western Europe.

1.69 _____ The Inquisition sought out heretics for punishment.

1.70 _____ Although the church was a powerful force, the kings of Europe were always more powerful than it was.

Monasteries. Monasteries appeared very early and developed slowly, but they were probably the most helpful institutions during the Middle Ages. They cared for the people and tried to make their lives easier.

Through the work of monks in the monasteries the church preserved ancient literature. Monks painstakingly copied old manuscripts, spending endless hours in the monastic **scriptorium** creating beautiful, illuminated manuscripts, many of which were artistic masterpieces. Thus ancient knowledge was preserved and available to students when universities came into being.

Besides preserving manuscripts, the monks taught better methods of agriculture, cared for the poor and the sick, and conducted church activities. A traveler was always sure of a safe place to spend the night if he came upon a monastery.

Toward the end of the Middle Ages, Franciscan and Dominican monks appeared. They had no monastery, for they took an oath of poverty. They traveled from place to place teaching and helping wherever they could and trusting in God to provide food, clothing, and shelter.

Crusades. The Church ordered the crusades at the request of the emperor of the Byzantine Empire in the eleventh century. Their mission was to recapture the Holy Land and particularly their Holy City, Jerusalem, from the Seljuk Turks. The Seljuk Turks were Muslims who had overrun southwest Asia and were beginning to move toward Europe. The Byzantine Empire was too weak to stop them.

The crusaders were unable to defeat the Turks, although for a short while they did regain Jerusalem. More important than the crusades themselves was the fact that products found in the Middle East and brought back to Europe were most desirable. Demand for these products stimulated trade, which in turn touched off the growth of towns and cities.

The church grew and prospered after the decline of the Roman Empire. By 1500 it was the leading power in Europe. Change, however, was near. The start of the Reformation was less than twenty years away.

| Monk working on script in scriptorium

Answer the following questions.

1.71 What was the purpose of the crusades?

_____

1.72 What was one important result of the crusades on life in medieval Europe?

_____

1.73 How did the Franciscan and Dominican monks differ from other monks of the Middle Ages?

_____

_____

1.74 What were three activities that took place in the medieval monastery?

a. _____

b. _____

c. _____

1.75 What was the name of the Holy City captured by the Seljuk Turks? _____

Review the material in this section in preparation for the Self Test. The Self Test will check your mastery of this particular section. The items missed on this Self Test will indicate specific areas where restudy is needed for mastery.

SELF TEST 1

Match these items (each answer, 2 points).

1.01	_____ Hammurabi	a. settled in Canaan
1.02	_____ pharaohs	b. Greek poet, author of the *Iliad*
1.03	_____ Genghis Khan	c. drove the Moors from Spain
1.04	_____ Mesopotamia	d. put down a Hebrew rebellion
1.05	_____ Ferdinand and Isabella	e. Egyptian rulers who where considered divine
1.06	_____ Homer	f. "land between two rivers"
1.07	_____ Alexander the Great	g. codified the laws of Babylon
1.08	_____ Peloponnesian War	h. conflict between Athens and Sparta
1.09	_____ Crete	i. origin of Greek civilization
1.010	_____ Abraham	j. Mongol warrior who invaded China
		k. spread Greek culture through the Middle East

Complete the following sentences (each answer, 3 points).

1.011 England was attacked many times in the early Middle Ages by warriors from Scandinavia called _____ .

1.012 Charlemagne was emperor of a land that was roughly the same as the modern country of _____ .

1.013 The king who united Southern England was named _____ .

1.014 The French ruler who invaded and ruled over England after 1066 was _____ .

1.015 Under the feudal system someone who received land in return for his support was called a _____ .

1.016 A parcel of land given by a noble to a lesser noble in exchange for loyalty and money in the Middle Ages was called a _____ .

1.017 Most people in the Middle Ages worked hard in the fields and were called _____ .

1.018   Minstrels and troubadours were known in the Middle Ages for their _____.

1.019   The two most important literary men of the Middle Ages were

a. _____ and b. _____ .

1.020   Late medieval architecture was called _____ .

Answer true or false (each answer, 1 point).

1.021   _____   Marco Polo was the first Chinese to visit Europe during the Middle Ages.

1.022   _____   Bronze is a mixture of iron and zinc.

1.023   _____   The empire of Alexander the Great began to crumble in part because Alexander did not pick a leader to follow him after he died.

1.024   _____   Plebeians were the common people of Rome.

1.025   _____   Antony and Cleopatra were defeated at the Battle of Actium in 31 B.C.

1.026   _____   Pax Romano was a Roman emperor who followed Diocletian to the throne.

1.027   _____   Jesus was born in Bethlehem during the reign of the emperor Augustus.

1.028   _____   The ancient Chinese had a highly developed system of government, which required formal education.

1.029   _____   Latin was the language of Egypt.

1.030   _____   The religion of most ancient civilizations was polytheistic.

Write the letter for the correct answer on each line (each answer, 2 points).

1.031 The feudal system dealt primarily with people at the _____ of the medieval social structure.

    a. top   b. middle   c. bottom   d. outside

1.032 Under the feudal system all of the land was owned by the _____ .

    a. manor   b. nobles   c. church   d. king

1.033 The *Canterbury Tales* were written by _____ .

    a. Dante   b. Chaucer   c. minstrels   d. Trivium

1.034 The papacy was moved from Rome to France during the _____ .

    a. Hundred Years War   b. Avignon Captivity

    c. Quadrivium   d. Holy Roman Empire

1.035 Campaigns to recapture the Holy Land during the Middle Ages were called _____ .

    a. Crusades   b. Inquisitions   c. Parliaments   d. Restorations

1.036 A nation which did not become unified until the nineteenth century was _____ .

    a. Turkey   b. Germany   c. Ireland   d. France

1.037 Cycles were groups of medieval _____ .

    a. songs   b. poems   c. plays   d. dances

1.038 Most medieval music was composed for _____ .

    a. monasteries   b. dramas   c. churches   d. wagon plays

1.039 The Old Testament of the Bible was God's gift through the _____ .

    a. Babylonians   b. Nicenes   c. popes   d. Hebrews

1.040 The Hebrews were the descendants of _____ .

    a. Canaan   b. Abraham   c. Jacob   d. Diaspora

2. RENAISSANCE AND REFORMATION

Beginning in Italy and spreading slowly to all parts of the European continent, the Renaissance came to Europe. The term *Renaissance* means *rebirth*. It was a time of new awareness of the classical, that is, the Greek and Roman spirit that had lain dormant throughout the Middle Ages. It was a time of learning, exploration, expansion, and social change.

Section Objectives

Review these objectives. When you have completed this section, you should be able to:

7. Point out the differences between the Middle Ages and the Renaissance.
8. Describe the politics in the major European countries during the Renaissance.
9. List the highlights of Renaissance arts and sciences.
10. Explain the Reformation.
11. Show how religious conflicts led to wars.
12. Define *absolutism*.
13. Show the development of the strongest nations in Europe.
14. Define mercantilism.
15. Trace the travels of European explorers and their claims in the New World.

Vocabulary

Study these words to enhance your learning success in this section.

hypothesize   indulgences

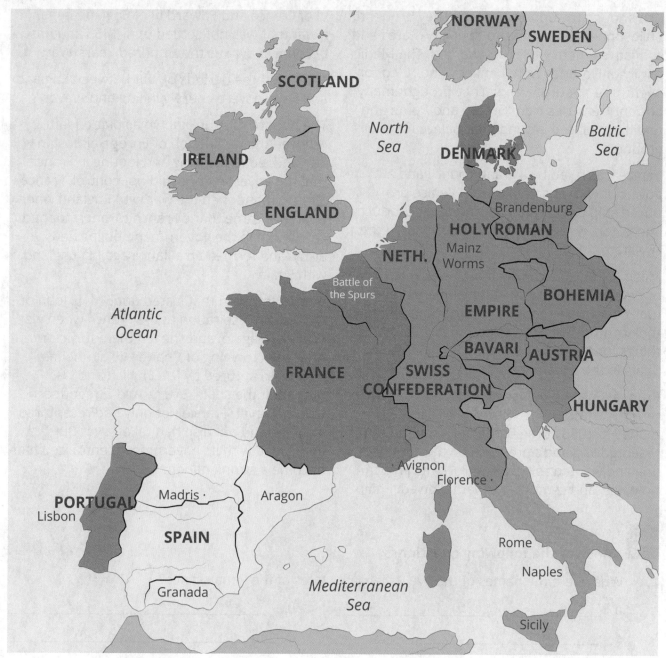

| European Nations in the 16th Century

POLITICS

The Renaissance began when trade increased at the end of the Middle Ages. Cities grew and prospered. Wealthy families had time for education and leisure activities. The Renaissance lasted in Northern Italy longer than it did anywhere else, and from there it spread to Northern Europe.

Italy. While nation-states with strong kings were forming in the rest of Europe, Italy was divided into city-states: Rome, Venice, Milan, Florence and Genoa. Of these city-states, Venice was the wealthiest. It had a fleet of over three thousand merchant ships. In all of these cities, bankers and merchants grew rich enough to support the arts. They brought philosophers and artists to their city-states and sponsored them while they worked. The Medici family of Florence were bankers who ruled for over three hundred years. They brought many ancient treasures from Greece and Rome and had them placed around their palaces and grounds.

Venice was ruled by a grand council and a governor with absolute power. Venice produced ship parts, cannons, and other products. There, too, wealthy merchants dominated the city-state.

Milan sold textiles and armor. It was ruled under a dictatorship for a long time but eventually became a republic, and the Sforza family took control. The Sforzas accomplished many things for Milan, but Milan was conquered by Spain in the early sixteenth century.

France. England owned a great deal of French territory through the victory of William of Normandy in 1066 at the Battle of Hastings. France resented England's presence on the continent. England wanted to keep control of its French holdings, and centuries of war followed. Philip

VI of France and Edward III of England began a war that was not settled until 1453 and has become known as the Hundred Years' War.

The first three periods of war between England and France were entirely in England's favor.

The bubonic plague, known as black death, reduced the population of Europe almost in half and led to pillaging and looting in France that the government could not control. France almost abandoned the war with England when Charles V came to the French throne, stopped corruption in the government, built a new army, and formed an alliance against England with Spain.

A truce followed that lasted until 1415. Joan of Arc was an inspiration to the French when war broke out again, and she led them to victory. After the crowning of Charles VII at Rheims, Joan was captured by the English and was burned at the stake. By the mid-fifteenth century, however, France not only had recaptured all of its land but also had taken over Burgundy and with its government centralized had become a strong nation.

Answer the following questions.

2.1 What were the names of the five Italian city-states of the Renaissance?

a. _____   b. _____

c. _____   d. _____

e. _____

2.2 Which two countries fought in the Hundred Years' War?

a. _____

b. _____

2.3 In which Italian city was the Medici family powerful? _____

2.4 Who led the French to victory in battle and was later burned at the stake by the English?

_____

2.5 What does the word *Renaissance* mean? _____

England. England was farther ahead in building a strong nation by the fourteenth century than other European countries. Citizens had more rights in England. They had a jury system. The Magna Carta had limited the king's power since 1215, and by 1295 the House of Commons had been established. England was far from a democracy, but the foundations for a parliamentary form of government had been laid.

Edward III in the mid-fourteenth century unified England in order to fight the war with France. Parliament grew in importance during his reign, and it became his chief source of raising money.

At Edward's death the country was thrown into a question of succession to the throne. The War of the Roses followed, which resulted in the great line of Tudor kings in England. The Tudors worked with Parliament although they were able to manipulate Parliament into doing what they wanted. The Tudors brought strong centralized government to England.

Spain. Under King Ferdinand and Queen Isabella, Spain drove the Moors and Jews out in 1492. Very firm in their Catholic belief, the monarchs insisted that all Muslims and Jews either leave or become converted to Catholicism. Spain also financed the voyage of Christopher Columbus to the New World in 1492.

 Answer true or false.

2.6 _____ By the fourteenth century citizens of Spain had more rights than those of any other country in Europe.

2.7 _____ The War of the Roses in England resulted in the Tudor line of English kings.

2.8 _____ The voyage of Christopher Columbus to the New World was financed by the same king and queen who expelled the Moors and Jews from Spain.

2.9 _____ The Magna Carta limited the power of the Tudors in England since 1215.

2.10 _____ Spain in the 1400s was a Roman Catholic country.

ARTS AND SCIENCES

The Renaissance brought a new desire for learning to Europe. With the invention of the Gutenberg printing press, books could be printed relatively inexpensively; and more people could buy and read them. A new movement, called *humanism*, appeared during the fourteenth century in Italy. Its focus was on man and his life in this world, and it led to a revival of interest in the ancient Greek and Latin cultures.

Literature. Beginning in Italy and spreading through Spain, France, Northern Europe, and England, many changes took place in literature and thought. These changes were spread by the invention of the movable-type printing press.

In Italy the "father of humanism" was Petrarch. Petrarch tried to encourage a spread of interest in the classics, that is, in the art and literature of ancient Greece and Rome. He has also been called the first "modern man" because of his interest in the humanities and because of his methods, which differed greatly from those of medieval scholars. Petrarch wrote over three hundred love sonnets, which were imitated by European poets. Another Italian, Boccaccio, was the first Renaissance storyteller. Some of his writings provided models for Chaucer's tales. Boccaccio's masterpiece was the *Decameron*.

A third Italian, Niccolo Machiavelli, was a diplomat, dramatist, historian, and poet who dreamed of unifying Italy. He wrote a manual for rulers called *The Prince*, which encouraged unethical and sometimes cruel means for a ruler to remain in power. Because of his realistic look at politics, Machiavelli has been called the "father of political science."

In Northern Europe humanists utilized the teachings of early Christianity. These teachings were known as *Christian humanism*, and they attempted to restore purity to Christianity. Erasmus, the greatest scholar of his time in Europe, wrote *The Praise of Folly* to portray man's nature and the problems of the church. Erasmus ridiculed man's interest in war and the sale of **indulgences** by the church.

Great French writers of the Renaissance included Rabelais, a monk who was also a Christian humanist, physician, and scholar. He wrote satires on medieval institutions and customs, and he believed in the value of education. Montaigne, another French scholar, developed the personal essay into a new literary form.

England produced many Renaissance writers. Sir Thomas More, an outstanding Christian humanist, wrote *Utopia*, his picture of an ideal society compared to the corruption of the world around him. Sir Francis Bacon, another writer, wrote *The New Atlantis*, which also described an ideal world. English drama achieved prominence with the works of Christopher Marlowe and William Shakespeare, who is considered the greatest literary figure in the English language. Shakespeare wrote thirty-eight known plays.

Spanish writers of the Renaissance included poets, dramatists, and novelists. The most outstanding dramatist of the period was Lope de Vega, who had served in the Spanish Armada

| Michaelangelo's *David*

against England and who had been a member of the government. His plays were usually on historical or religious subjects.

Miguel de Cervantes was the most outstanding contributor to Spanish literature. His *Don Quixote de la Mancha*, a satire on chivalry, is still widely read today and was the basis of a contemporary American musical.

Painting. One of the greatest of the Renaissance artists was an Italian, Leonardo da Vinci, who painted the famed *Mona Lisa* and *The Last Supper*. Da Vinci has been called the "universal man." His mind inquired into everything, and he conceived several modern technological developments centuries before they were imagined possible by anyone else. He studied botany, physiology, mathematics, and sculpture. He drew plans for an airplane, a battle tank, and a parachute.

Another Italian, Michelangelo, is considered by many to be the greatest artist of all time. He was not only a painter and sculptor but also an architect, engineer, and poet. Michelangelo created almost three hundred and fifty fresco figures for the ceiling of the Sistine Chapel in Rome depicting such scenes as the "Creation of Adam" from Genesis. Thousands still view these paintings each year. As a sculptor, Michelangelo produced the *Pieta*, *David*, and *Moses*.

Raphael was another great Italian painter. Blending classical culture and Christianity, his most famous painting is the *Sistine Madonna*.

Raphael's portrait painting achieved new heights of popularity. Art scholars consider him one of the greatest Renaissance painters.

Painting also flourished in Flanders. The Flemish school of painting included Jan and Hubert van Eyck and Peter Brueghel. Unlike the Van Eycks, who painted three-dimensional figures and landscapes, Brueghel concentrated on landscapes and scenes from common life. *The Harvesters* is one of his realistic peasant scenes.

German painters included Albrecht Dürer, who led the German Renaissance school of painting, and Hans Holbein, who was court painter to the king of England. Holbein painted the famous portraits of Henry VIII and Sir Thomas More.

✏️ **Match these items.**

2.11 _____	Petrarch	a. *Don Quixote*
2.12 _____	Erasmus	b. *Mona Lisa*
2.13 _____	Cervantes	c. invented movable type printing press
2.14 _____	Michelangelo	d. designed the Vatican
2.15 _____	da Vinci	e. greatest figure in English literature
2.16 _____	Gutenberg	f. *Utopia*
2.17 _____	Sir Thomas More	g. "father of political science"
2.18 _____	Machiavelli	h. a monk who satirized medieval institutions
2.19 _____	Shakespeare	i. The Praise of Folly
2.20 _____	Rabelais	j. "father of humanism"
		k. Sistine Chapel

Architecture. Three types of architecture are clearly seen among buildings erected during the Renaissance period. *Romanesque* architecture originated earlier but was still being used at the beginning of the Renaissance. It was characterized by thick, heavy walls with small windows set well back. Many Romanesque churches were built throughout Northern Europe. They are dark and gloomy. Ceilings and windows are supported by low, wide arches.

Gothic is the style of the great cathedrals of Europe. Notre Dame in Paris is one of the best examples. These buildings are constructed in the shape of a cross. They have high, vaulted ceilings, pointed roofs, and stained-glass windows. Spires, steeples, pointed arches, and flying buttresses are easily seen. These buildings are decorated with elaborate carvings and enormous windows of stained glass famed for their spectacular beauty.

Byzantine architecture is very elaborate. Buildings are colorful and consist of complex domes and vaults set over a square or rectangular base. St. Sophia's in Constantinople (Istanbul) is beautifully decorated with mosaics and very colorful paintings. St. Basil's in Russia is of a similar type.

Science. The Renaissance observed the growth of the scientific method. Scientific experiments were carried on in which observable proof was necessary before a conclusion was judged to be true. For example, that blood circulates through the human body was **hypothesized** long before scientific experiments proved it. Today, because of those experiments, we know that blood travels through the body, where it goes, and why.

The new science was immediately put to work. In Italy, Leonardo da Vinci used it to develop canals with locks to divert rivers, to design buildings, and to build new towns. Copernicus proved that the sun rather than the earth is the center of the solar system. The work of Galileo led to laws of gravity. Sir Isaac Newton wrote laws of gravity and motion.

 Complete the following sentences.

2.21 Three types of architecture seen among the great buildings of the Renaissance were

a. _____ , b. _____ , and c. _____ .

2.22 The Renaissance witnessed the growth of the scientific method, in which observable

_____ was necessary before a conclusion was true.

2.23 A famous Renaissance artist who also built canals and towns was _____ .

2.24 That the sun, rather than the earth, is the center of our solar system, was shown by

_____ .

2.25 Both Galileo and Sir Isaac Newton wrote laws concerning _____ .

REFORMATION

The Reformation spread throughout Western Europe in the sixteenth and seventeenth centuries. It began as a protest by such religious leaders as Martin Luther and John Calvin against corruption and abuses that had arisen in the Roman Catholic Church. The Reformation spread to England where it caused enormous political and social upheavals. The English king, Henry VIII, took over the church and established the Anglican Church as the official religion. England in the next years became either a Protestant or a Catholic country, depending upon the religion of the reigning monarch. Strong feelings over religious issues ultimately resulted in a series of European wars.

Reformers. A scholarly English theologian, John Wycliffe, was concerned with the spreading corruption in the Roman Catholic Church. In his writings he denounced clerical abuses and recommended drastic reforms. He questioned the authority of the pope, and he denied the right of a ruler to demand obedience on the claim that it was God's will (the "divine right" of kings).

In 1378 the papal schism produced two rival popes when French cardinals elected a French pope because they disliked the pope in Rome. Each pope claimed authority by divine right. This disgusted Wycliffe even further, leading him to attack the office of the pope and the sacraments. He believed that the Bible was the only true guide for Christian conduct. His main contribution was that he and his followers made the first major translation of the Bible into English. Wycliffe was eventually banished as a heretic.

Wycliffe's followers, known as *Lollards*, were persecuted. Many were hanged or forced to escape the country. Nevertheless, Wycliffe influenced reformers everywhere. He was considered the first true English reformer.

John Huss, a Bohemian priest, attacked the church offices, but not the sacraments. He too was disgusted when, as a result of the papal schism, a third pope denounced the other two, and claimed divine authority. Huss was declared a heretic, excommunicated from the church, and burned at the stake. After his death his followers broke from the church and established the Unity of Brethren, or Moravian Church, which could be called the first Protestant church.

Martin Luther was trained early to become an Augustinian monk. As a successful professor at the University of Wittenberg in Germany, Luther realized that faith in God would save man and that faith could be attained through reading the Bible. This idea was in conflict with the church's sale of indulgences and the Catholic belief that both faith and good works lead to salvation. Disturbed by the lack of faith among monks he knew and by the worldliness of church officers, Luther protested against church teachings.

On October 31, 1517, Martin Luther nailed his famous Ninety-Five Theses to the door of the church at Wittenberg. Luther's ideas included the belief that the pope could not forgive sinners, but was only God's representative on earth. Luther had no idea the effect his action would have. His theses were published and debated everywhere. People stopped buying indulgences, and the clergy complained to the pope.

Luther was called before a papal council to explain his beliefs. There he expanded them, attacking the mass and the use of Latin in the service, saying that all believers should partake of the Lord's Supper. Luther claimed that marriage was not a sacrament and that it belonged to all people, not just Christians. Luther was excommunicated by the pope. When he received his decree of excommunication, he burned it. He was forced to escape in disguise to save his life.

Eventually Luther was able to return. He and his followers, known as Protestants, formed their own church. The Protestants simplified the church service, omitted the mass, and eliminated monastic orders. Lutheranism spread rapidly leading to revolts and violence in many places, which did not end for many years.

A Swiss priest, Ulrich Zwingli, heard of Martin Luther's beliefs and found them to be like his own. Encouraged by Luther's example, Zwingli began to preach in Zurich. Zwingli favored a type of religion without saints, fasting, or celibate priests. Under Zwingli, Zurich became a theocracy, which meant that it had a religious form of government.

Another religious group in Zurich was known as the *Anabaptists* because they believed in adult baptism and could not find a Scriptural basis for infant baptism. Rather than join other Protestant Movements the Anabaptists, led by Conrad Grebel, formed their own groups in Germany, the Netherlands, and Switzerland.

Anabaptists believed in separation of church and state. They believed in peace and opposed war. They opposed taking oaths. They were

| Famous Reformers of Europe including John Calvin, Ulrich Zwingli, Guillaume Farel, Théodore de Bèze, and John Knox.

persecuted for their beliefs by Protestants and Catholics alike and many were put to death.

John Calvin was a French Protestant who left France to avoid persecution. Calvin brought logic and organization to the ideas of Protestantism.

In 1536 Calvin published Institutes of the Christian Religion, which set forth his beliefs. Calvin believed faith to be all important. He believed the Bible was the only authority for men to live by. He denied the Catholic Church and favored a simplified church service. Calvin believed certain individuals—the elect—had been chosen at the Creation by God to be saved.

Eventually, Calvin became the leader of a theocracy in Geneva. A strict believer, he prohibited such activities as dancing, gambling, and wearing colorful or ornamental apparel. Many Calvinists were extreme in their religious zeal. Some citizens of Geneva were banished for their real or imagined heresy, and a few were actually put to death for refusing to accept all of Calvin's beliefs.

John Knox in Scotland established the Presbyterian Church. Knox, a former Catholic priest, became a Protestant minister in England. Knox fled England to Geneva where he was influenced by Calvin. Eventually returning to Scotland, he established his own church.

Write the letter for the correct answer on each line.

2.26 Martin Luther was trained as _____ .

a. a mathematics tutor   b. an Augustinian monk

c. an experimental scientist   d. an archbishop

2.27 The Ninety-Five Theses were _____ .

a. a reading list   b. indulgences   c. sacraments   d. proposals

2.28 The papal schism in 1378 produced two _____ .

a. popes   b. Protestant churches

c. sacraments   d. divine rights

2.29 The first Protestant church was formed by followers _____ .

a. Martin Luther   b. Pope Leo II   c. John Wycliffe   d. John Huss

2.30 Followers of Wycliffe were known as _____ .

a. papists   b. Protestants   c. Lollards   d. Wycliffites

2.31 John Wycliffe was _____ .

a. English   b. German   c. Italian   d. French

2.32 Martin Luther believed that faith in God would save man and that faith could be attained

through _____ .

a. the sale of indulgences   b. reading the Bible

c. trust in God   d. good works

Answer true or false.

2.33 _____ Anabaptists believed in baptizing all young children according to their interpretation of the Bible.

2.34 _____ John Calvin did not care how people lived their lives so long as they read the Bible.

2.35 _____ A theocracy is a government based on religious principles.

2.36 _____ Zurich was a theocracy under Ulrich Zwingli.

2.37 _____ Calvin believed baptism to be the most important factor in salvation.

2.38 _____ John Knox established the Presbyterian Church in Scotland.

England. England experienced some heresy in the sixteenth century but no movement for reform such as the rest of Europe was experiencing. There was anti-papal feeling, however. Separation of church and state was encouraged because the pope had involved the church in wars and politics. Corruption among the English clergy was widespread, and public opinion was turning against it as a result.

King Henry VIII used Parliament to attack papal power in England to force the pope to grant his wishes. Catherine of Aragon, Henry's wife, had not given him a male heir to continue his dynasty. He wanted to dissolve his marriage to Catherine and marry Anne Boleyn. Henry appealed to the pope to annul his marriage. The pope, Clement VII, would not grant Henry's wish. Henry, arrogant and headstrong, decided to bypass the pope. He appointed his own representative, Thomas Cranmer, Archbishop of Canterbury and head of the highest ecclesiastical, or church, court. Then Henry asked Cranmer for his annulment, which Cranmer granted. Henry married Anne, and an angry Pope Clement excommunicated him.

Henry beheaded Anne when she left no male heirs. He married several more times and had a total of seven wives. In 1534 he had Parliament pass the "Act of Supremacy" which made him head of the Church of England, called the *Anglican* Church. The Anglican Church was to be the same as the Catholic Church from which it had separated, except that it no longer accepted the pope as leader.

As head of the church in England, Henry closed the monasteries and seized their lands, adding to his own wealth and that of his supporters. He persecuted Catholics and Lutherans, torturing and executing many. However, he authorized an English translation of the Bible. Fundamentally he disapproved of allowing the people to interpret the Scriptures, but he allowed them the Bible in their own language.

Reform. The counter-Reformation, or Catholic Reformation, actually had its beginning before Luther's Ninety-Five Theses. Later, as a result of Protestant pressures, the need for church reforms was intensified. The major figure in Spanish church reform was the Franciscan Cardinal Ximenez. He was the confessor of Queen Isabella, who was impressed with his wisdom and knowledge. Finally he was appointed a cardinal and chancellor of the state.

Despite his high office, Ximenez lived a simple life, going barefoot and wearing simple robes. Ximenez was responsible for the first printed edition of the Bible in the original languages— Hebrew Old Testament and Greek New Testament.

Spain was a center for Catholicism in the sixteenth century. It was also the strongest European military power of its time. Out of this Catholic stronghold grew a religious order, *The Society of Jesus*. Its founder was Ignatius of Loyola. Loyola was a soldier who underwent conversion and became a priest. Members of his society, called *Jesuits*, were organized in military fashion. Each member obeyed his superior. Only members of the upper class with intelligence, education, physical fitness, and character were eligible to join. The Jesuits spread Catholicism among infidels, Protestants, and Catholics who had strayed from the basic Catholic beliefs.

The Council of Trent in 1545 paved the way for church reform. The council was convened by Charles V to deal with Lutheran Protestants. It encouraged more discipline within the clergy and insisted on a abolishing church abuses. The council recognized the pope as the authority on doctrine. Catholic doctrines concerning the seven sacraments, indulgences, purgatory, and the saints were reaffirmed. One of the most important results of the Council of Trent was that it tended to unify the church and encouraged the clergy.

HISTORY & GEOGRAPHY 1010

LIFEPAC TEST

NAME _____

DATE _____

SCORE _____

HISTORY & GEOGRAPHY 1010: LIFEPAC TEST

Write the letter for the correct answer on each line (each answer, 2 points).

1. In ancient times the "land between two rivers" was called _____ .
   a. Greece   b. Mesopotamia   c. Canaan   d. Egypt

2. The Macedonian leader who spread Greek culture throughout the Middle East was _____ .
   a. Julius Caesar   b. King Menes   c. Hammurabi   d. Alexander the Great

3. In the feudal system of the Middle Ages, someone who received land in exchange for his support was called a _____ .
   a. vassal   b. troubadour   c. fief   d. peasant

4. Warriors from Scandinavia who attacked England in the early Middle Ages were called _____ .
   a. Mongols   b. Normans   c. Vikings   d. Goths

5. The Italian who walked to China and brought back fabulous stories of what he saw there was _____ .
   a. Visigoth   b. Homer   c. Leonardo   d. Marco Polo

6. Jesus was born in Bethlehem during the time of _____ rule there.
   a. Roman   b. Jewish   c. Greek   d. Chinese

7. The emperor of Babylonia who codified the laws of his country was _____ .
   a. pharaoh   b. Hammurabi   c. Nile   d. Shinar

8. One result of the crusades was that the demand grew in Europe for products from _____ .
   a. Babylon   b the East   c. Israel   d. England

9. The emperor who divided the Roman Empire into two parts to make it easier to rule was _____ .
   a. Diocletian   b. Homer   c. *Pax Romano*   d. Augustus

10. Most medieval music was composed for the _____ .
    a. home   b. wagon plays   c. church   d. theater

Complete the following sentences (each answer, 3 points).

11. The best example of an absolute king, who wrecked France with his wars and religious intolerance, was _____ .

12. The English explorer who landed on the coast of Nova Scotia and gave England a claim to the North American continent was _____ .

13. The first successful British settlement in the New World was at _____ .

14. King Henry VIII founded the Church of _____ .

15. Many scholars consider _____ to be the greatest English author in history.

16. Copernicus said the center of the solar system is the _____ .

17. Lollards were followers of _____ .

18. An Augustinian monk who began the Reformation with his Ninety-Five Theses was _____ .

19. During the civil war in England, the Puritan supporters of Oliver Cromwell were called _____ .

20. Renaissance means _____ .

Answer true or false (each answer, 1 point).

21. _____ The Bill of Rights was part of the first American Constitution.

22. _____ Charlemagne ruled in what is now France.

23. _____ Plebeians were the common people of Rome.

24. _____ *The Canterbury Tales* were written by Dante.

25. _____ Napoleon died in France at the peak of his power.

26. _____ The French National Assembly passed the Declaration of the Rights of Man, which was based on ideas from the American Revolution.

27. _____ Under the theory of mercantilism, nations became powerful by stockpiling money.

28. _____ The purpose of the Federal Trade Commission is to allow corporations in the United States to grow as big as they can without interference.

29. _____ The Industrial Revolution has been a blessing for all people since it began.

30. _____ The Triple Alliance prior to World War I was made up of Germany, Italy, and Austria-Hungary.

Match these items (each answer, 2 points).

31. _____ Archduke Ferdinand

32. _____ MacArthur

33. _____ Homer

34. _____ Joan of Arc

35. _____ Calvin

36. _____ Magellan

37. _____ Petrarch

38. _____ Truman

39. _____ Jefferson

40. _____ Guy Fawkes

a. author of the *Iliad*

b. burned for fighting the English

c. assassination set off World War I

d. wrote the *Divine Comedy*

e. tried to blow up the English Parliament and the king

f. ordered atomic bomb dropped on Japan

g. thought some people were already chosen by God to be saved

h. began a journey around the world

i. commanded forces in the Pacific

j. wrote the Declaration of Independence

k. "father of humanism"

Other methods by the pope to halt the spread of Protestantism were the *concordats*, the *Index*, and the *Inquisition*. Concordats were made with the various Catholic rulers of Europe. The monarchs were given more freedom from papal control in return for supporting Catholicism. These concordats helped to prevent Southern Europe from supporting Protestantism.

Pope Paul IV drew up the Index, which was a list of books that Catholics were forbidden to read. A special church court called the Inquisition was established in the thirteenth century to deal with heretics. The Inquisition was later used to deal with anyone suspected of being in disagreement with the church. The Spanish Inquisition became notorious because it used torture and executions to achieve its ends.

Complete these sentences.

2.39 Members of the Society of Jesus were called _____.

2.40 The founder of the Society of Jesus was _____ .

2.41 Henry VIII of England wanted to dissolve his marriage to Catherine of Aragon because

_____

_____ .

2.42 After Henry VIII the Church of England was also called the _____ Church.

2.43 The Council of Trent in 1545 paved the way for church _____ .

2.44 The major Spanish figure in reform of the Catholic Church was a confessor to Queen Isabella named Cardinal _____.

2.45 In 1534 King Henry VIII had Parliament pass the _____ , which made him the head of the Church of England.

Conflict. Catholics and Protestants in Europe were each convinced their beliefs were the only way to salvation. Each group accused the other of heresy, and civil wars broke out. Torn by religious strife, France was divided into three groups of religious thought. One was the Huguenots, or French Calvinists. A second group included Catholics who wanted Catholicism as the national religion. A third group was made up of Catholics more interested in politics than religion.

France was officially Catholic, but Huguenots were allowed to practice their religion without persecution. Disputes between Protestants and Catholics arose, however, culminating in the *Massacre of Saint Bartholomew*, in which ten thousand Protestants in Paris were killed.

The Netherlands in the sixteenth century was made up of seventeen provinces including what is now Belgium. The people were divided by language and religion. The Dutch-speaking people of the northern provinces became Calvinistic, but the Flemish-speaking people of the south remained Catholic.

When Spain took over the Netherlands in 1555, the people rebelled. Mobs spread destruction among the country's Catholic churches. A special court was set up to deal with these Protestant rebels, and many were put to death.

The Thirty Years' War in Germany grew out of religious and political differences. Religious intolerance combined with commercial rivalry resulted in unstable alliances between former enemies to oppose a greater threat—the Hapsburgs. By 1635 the Hapsburg rulers of Spain and of the Holy Roman Empire united against Protestant Germany, Holland, France, and Sweden. After thirteen more years of war, a truce was agreed upon. *The Peace of Westphalia* contained the details of the agreements that ended the war. It brought an end to religious and political turmoil.

Answer true or false.

2.46 _____ The Index was established in the thirteenth century to deal with heretics.

2.47 _____ Thousands of Catholics were killed in the Massacre of Saint Bartholomew.

2.48 _____ Huguenots were French Calvinists.

2.49 _____ The Peace of Westphalia ended the Thirty Years' War.

2.50 _____ When Spain took over the Netherlands in 1555, mobs spread destruction among the country's Protestant churches.

ABSOLUTISM

In the period following the Renaissance and the Reformation in Europe, two theories predominated, one political and one economic. The political theory was *absolutism*, which held that a strong central government was necessary for efficient rule and prosperity. Along with absolutism went the divine right of kings, which said the king, who was chosen by God, was absolute in his powers and responsible only to God.

Mercantilism was the economic extension of absolute government. The government controlled a nation's economy and ruled over every aspect of people's lives.

England. The Tudor family and the first Tudor king, Henry VII, came to the throne of England in 1485 at the end of the War of the Roses. The middle classes in England wanted strong leadership, and the Tudors gave it to them. Thus, under the Tudors, Parliament was little more than a rubber stamp for the monarchs' actions. The Tudors reigned with little real opposition, although never with the absolute authority seen at the same time in France.

The two most powerful Tudor monarchs were Henry VIII and Elizabeth I. Henry came to the throne in 1509. During his reign he broke away entirely from the Roman Catholic Church when the pope would not annul his marriage to Catherine of Aragon. He formed the Church of England, or Anglican Church, and became its head. Henry's private life greatly influenced political history in England. He also established the Reformation in England. Henry was cruel and domineering, but he understood his people and had their respect and confidence.

Elizabeth I came to the throne in 1558. She avoided foreign involvements and war although war with Spain did come in 1588. Philip II of Spain sent the Spanish Armada against England for three reasons. First, he resented England's interference in the Netherlands. Second, Philip was a Catholic, and he wanted to force

| Henry VIII of England

England's return to the Catholic Church through military means. Third, and most important, Spain wanted to stop English interference in its New World trade.

Philip sent the Spanish Armada, a fleet of 130 ships, against England in July, 1588. An English fleet under Admiral Lord Charles Howard badly damaged the Armada in a battle lasting over a week. The Spanish retreated and were further mauled by storms in the North Sea. Less than half of Philip's "Invincible Armada" returned to Spain. England remained independent and Protestant. The power of Spain declined, and the way was open for England to become a major power in the New World.

Elizabeth's chief contributions to England were the relative peace and prosperity of her reign. She ruled for forty-five years and brought stability to England. She was succeeded on the throne by her nearest heir, cousin James I, who was also James VI of Scotland.

James was the first of the Stuart kings. He was a Protestant with children, thus ensuring no religious struggles later for the throne. He thought of himself as a divine right king, however, and conflict between James and Parliament began almost immediately. James alienated Parliament and the people with his insistence that all power rested in his hands, having come to him as a gift from God. He believed that he could take away any individual's rights whenever he wished.

Parliament fought back, first by refusing James the money he always seemed to need. Merchants and manufacturers also sought to decrease the king's power, and they had become a powerful group with considerable economic influence. James was also opposed by the Puritans, who had hoped he would reform the Anglican Church. During this time of stress, the famous Gunpowder Plot took place. Guy Fawkes, a Catholic extremist, and his companions narrowly failed to blow up the king and Parliament with gunpowder in the Parliament building basement.

James died in 1625 and was succeeded by his son, Charles I. Like his father, Charles believed in divine right of kings. He also disliked the Puritans, who had become a powerful religious and social force. His fight with Parliament for money was almost continuous. In 1628 Parliament forced him to sign the *Petition of Right* before it would vote him the money he wanted. The Petition of Right stated that no one could be taxed without Parliament's consent, no one could be imprisoned without a trial, and no one could be forced to house soldiers in peacetime. Along with the Magna Carta, this document was one of the most important ones in the history of England's political system. Once his war with France was over, however, Charles ignored it.

Charles antagonized almost everyone. He persecuted Puritans. He used ancient and burdensome methods of taxation to raise money from his people. He tried to impose the episcopal system of church government and a new prayer book on Scotland. This action led to war with Scotland and a need for more money and more conflict with Parliament. Open conflict with Parliament was inevitable. Civil war in England broke out.

Supporters of Charles in the war were called *cavaliers*. These royalists were Catholics, moderate Anglicans, aristocracy, and conservative agricultural interests. Parliament's supporters were merchants and middle class, Presbyterians and Puritans. They were called *Roundheads* because their hair was cut short.

Oliver Cromwell emerged as leader of the Roundheads; and, when his forces won, he saw Charles as a threat to new order, Charles was beheaded in 1649. Cromwell's government did not last. Cromwell did not trust the common people. Elections were abolished, and the government became a military dictatorship. When Cromwell died, his son could not carry on; and the monarchy was restored to Charles's son, Charles II in 1658. Charles was fun-loving and earned the name the Merry Monarch. He was careful to stay on good terms with Parliament. Two major developments came out of his reign. First was the Habeas Corpus Act of 1679, which forbade imprisoning anyone without explaining why he was being held. Second was the emergence of political parties. Absolutism had lost its grip in England, apparently for all time.

Answer the following questions.

2.51 What was the theory called that held a king was chosen by God and was responsible to no one but God? _____

2.52 What was the name of the war in England that brought the Tudors to the throne?

_____

2.53 Who was the English king who broke away from the Roman Catholic Church and declared himself head of the Church of England? _____

2.54 What was the Spanish Armada? _____

_____

2.55 What happened to the Spanish Armada? _____

_____

2.56 Give three reasons why Philip II attacked England.

a. _____

b. _____

c. _____

2.57 Who was Guy Fawkes? _____

_____

Match these items.

2.58 _____ cavaliers

2.59 _____ Petition of Right

2.60 _____ Oliver Cromwell

2.61 _____ Charles I

2.62 _____ Roundheads

2.63 _____ Charles II

a. Roundhead leader

b. invaded Ireland

c. document limiting king's power

d. beheaded in 1649

e. Merry Monarch

f. supported the king

g. supported Parliament

| Versailles

France. The rise of absolutism was similar in France to that in England. French rulers had a Huguenot opposition almost as strong as the Puritans in England. France had a prosperous middle class to contend with the monarchs and the nobility. One major difference was that France faced constant threat of invasion from the outside.

In 1589 Henry III was assassinated, and he left no heir to the throne. The Huguenot leader, Henry of Navarre, declared himself king. French Catholics and Philip II of Spain refused to recognize him. War followed, after which Henry converted to Catholicism in the interest of peace. He was crowned Henry IV in 1594.

Although now a Catholic, Henry issued the *Edict of Nantes* in 1598 giving freedom of worship to the Huguenots. France became the first country in Europe to grant freedom to more than one religious group. Henry laid the foundations for France to become the strongest nation in Europe. He built canals and highways and promoted agriculture. His reign, although despotic, was intelligent and benevolent.

France almost plunged into disaster after the assassination of Henry IV when his eight-year old son gained the throne as Louis XIII. The mother of Louis, Marie de Medici, ruled in his place and nearly took the nation into war. Fortunately for France, Cardinal Richelieu became chief minister.

Richelieu increased French national strength. His goals were to make the king all-powerful in France and to make France supreme in Europe. He succeeded in both. He had little concern for the common people who bore the heavy taxes imposed to carry out his goals. They rejoiced at his death in 1642. Louis the XIII died a year later. His son, Louis XIV, succeeded him at the age of four. Louis' mother, Anne of Austria, acted as regent until he was 23 years old.

Louis XIV became the perfect example of the absolute king. He chose the sun as his official emblem to indicate that the glory of France came from him. His power was absolute. Louis continued the policies of Henry IV and Richelieu in consolidating national power at the expense of the nobles and local officials. He reorganized the army and strengthened the navy. His reign however, was repeatedly damaged by wars and his own religious intolerance. He revoked the Edict of Nantes and began to persecute the Huguenots.

Louis XIV lived in unheard-of personal luxury. His palace at Versailles could accommodate ten thousand people. It had hundreds of rooms, took thirty-two years to build, and required the labor of thirty-five thousand men to complete. All Europe followed the French example of the etiquette and ceremony established at Versailles.

Louis XIV was followed by dull, indecisive rulers who presided over French decline until the end of the eighteenth century and the French Revolution.

Mercantilism. Mercantilism was a system of government intervention to increase national trade and prosperity. By selling more than it bought, a nation stockpiled money that could be used to increase its influence, to build armies, and to control others. Mercantilism reached its peak between 1600 and 1700.

Complete the following sentences.

2.64 The two major goals of Cardinal Richelieu were a. _____ _____ and b. _____ .

2.65 In 1598 Henry IV of France gave freedom of worship to the Huguenots by issuing the document known as the _____ .

2.66 Louis XIII became king of France when he was _____ years old.

2.67 The emblem chosen by Louis XIV to represent himself was the _____ .

2.68 As absolute ruler of France, Louis XIV damaged his country by a. _____ and b. _____ .

2.69 Through the system of mercantilism, a nation tried to stockpile _____ which was used to increase its influence.

Exploration. The revival of trade in the late Middle Ages increased commerce between Europe and the East. All routes to the East were by both land and sea, however, making goods very expensive. Major nations began to search for a single sea route to the East. This search led indirectly to the exploration of the New World and claims on it by European countries.

First to seek the so-called Northwest Passage through the New World was the English explorer, John Cabot. He landed on the coast of Nova Scotia and gave England a claim to the entire continent. Sir Francis Drake, an English explorer and pirate, sailed up the west coasts of South and North America searching for the exit of the fabled Northwest Passage. Drake may have traveled as far north as Vancouver in his expedition.

Sailing for the Dutch, Henry Hudson made several attempts to find the passage. He discovered the Hudson River in New York, which is named for him.

The first successful settlement was at Jamestown, Virginia, in 1607, by the English. Plymouth and Massachusetts Bay were established in 1620 and 1621 respectively; and they were followed by others, which eventually became the original thirteen colonies. English colonies grew and became prosperous.

France's earliest effort was made by the explorer Verrazano in 1524. He explored the east coast from North Carolina to Newfoundland. In 1534 Jacques Cartier explored the St. Lawrence River hoping to find a way to China. Cartier claimed eastern North America, calling it New France, duplicating the English claim and paving the way for later conflict. Quebec was France's first New World colony. It was established in 1608 by Samuel de Champlain. It was soon followed by the founding of Montreal further upstream on the St. Lawrence River.

Bitter enemies in Europe, France and England took their ruinous wars with them to the New World. Conflict was inevitable as France moved westward to the Mississippi River valley, and England colonized eastern North America. In order to protect their territory from the English, the French built forts and made alliances with the nearby Native American people. The colonial duel lasted nearly a hundred years and climaxed in the Seven Years' War, also known as the French and Indian War. England emerged triumphant. France lost most of its colonies, its treasury was empty, and its trade was nearly ruined.

King Henry of Portugal, called the Navigator because of his desire to explore and his interest in the sea, established a school of navigation in 1415, which trained many Portuguese seamen and made Portugal a major power in the era of exploration. In 1487, Bartolomeu Dias sailed around the tip of Africa, proving the trip could be made by sea. In 1497, Vasco da Gama sailed around Africa to India establishing a major new sea route.

The first explorer to reach the New World was Christopher Columbus. He convinced King Ferdinand and Queen Isabella of Spain that he could sail west to find the East Indies and new riches. On October 12, 1492, he and his crew anchored at Watling Island in the Caribbean Sea. Columbus went on to discover the islands of Cuba and Hispaniola. Until the day he died, Columbus believed he had actually found the East Indies.

A Portuguese sailing under the flag of Spain, Ferdinand Magellan was responsible for the first voyage around the world. Although he was killed on the long, dangerous voyage in which most of his crew died, Magellan's name has been added to the list of the world's great explorers.

Spain believed great wealth could be obtained by conquering and exploiting the people of the New World. The Spaniard Hernando Cortez conquered the Aztecs of Mexico and their leader Montezuma. Through treachery and war Cortez took great wealth from the sincere natives who had trusted in him. Francisco Pizarro accomplished the same destruction among the Incas of Peru. Through lies, treachery, and cruelty he enslaved the Incas, killed their leaders, and took from them their gold and other treasure. However, Pizarro and many of his men were finally killed by fever and starvation in the swamps of Peru.

Spanish settlement in the New World began at the island of Hispaniola in the West Indies, spread quickly to the other islands, and then spread to South America and Mexico. By 1575 two hundred Spanish settlements had been established in the New World. Spanish colonies were strictly controlled by the Spanish government and the king of Spain. As it did in Spain itself, the Roman Catholic Church also exerted much control over New World settlers. Three main social classes were in the Spanish colonies.

The *peninsulares* were appointed by the king and sent to the New World directly from Spain. *Creoles* were aristocratic Spaniards born in the New World. People of mixed Spanish and Native American descent made up the third class, which was 80 percent of the population. Other groups in the Spanish colonies included people of mixed white and black heritage, Native Americans, and black people. These minority groups did most of the manual labor and lived as serfs or slaves.

Spanish power in the New World declined as precious metals were depleted. The Spanish had not invested their wealth in industry, education, or anything of lasting value. Years of inbreeding among Spanish royalty caused mental and physical deterioration of the Spanish kings. Weak kings encouraged corruption among civil workers which, along with wars, emptied the Spanish treasury.

Answer true or false.

2.70 _____ The French and Indian War was won by the French.

2.71 _____ Sir Francis Drake was the first explorer to land in Nova Scotia.

2.72 _____ The first successful English settlement in the New World was at Jamestown, Virginia.

2.73 _____ Verrazano explored the east coast from North Carolina to Newfoundland.

2.74 _____ King Henry of France was given the name the Navigator.

2.75 _____ Portugal was a major power during the Age of Exploration.

2.76 _____ Ferdinand Magellan was responsible for the first voyage around the world.

2.77 _____ Vasco da Gama found an all-sea route from Europe to India.

Match these items.

2.78 _____ Plymouth

2.79 _____ Pizarro

2.80 _____ Creole

2.81 _____ Cortez

2.82 _____ peninsulares

2.83 _____ Hispaniola

a. Spanish aristocrat born in New World

b. island where Spanish settlement began

c. conquered the West Indies

d. one of the first settlements in Jamestown

e. people appointed by the king and sent from Spain

f. enslaved the Incas

g. conquered the Aztecs

TEACHER CHECK _____ _____

initials   date

Review the material in this section in preparation for the Self Test. This Self Test will check your mastery of this particular section as well as your knowledge of the previous section.

SELF TEST 2

Match these items (each answer, 2 points).

2.01	_____ Joan of Arc	a. preached Luther's message in Zurich
2.02	_____ Ferdinand and Isabella	b. established the Presbyterian Church
2.03	_____ Petrarch	c. Ninety-Five Theses
2.04	_____ Leonardo da Vinci	d. "father of humanism"
2.05	_____ Gutenberg	e. painted *The Last Supper*
2.06	_____ Shakespeare	f. wrote the *Decameron*
2.07	_____ Copernicus	g. greatest English writer in history
2.08	_____ Martin Luther	h. said the sun was the center of the solar system
2.09	_____ Zwingli	i. banished the Moors and Jews from Spain
2.010	_____ John Knox	j. burned at the stake for aiding the French against the English
		k. invented the movable type printing press

Complete the following sentences (each answer, 3 points).

2.011 Followers of John Wycliffe, many of whom were hanged or forced to escape from England, were called _____ .

2.012 The papal schism of 1378, produced two _____ .

2.013 Anabaptists were Protestants who believed in adult _____ .

2.014 The Church of England, or Anglican Church, was founded by _____ .

2.015 Jesuits were members of the _____ .

2.016 A list of books that Roman Catholics were forbidden to read was called the _____ .

2.017 The Peace of Westphalia ended the _____ War.

2.018 The two most powerful Tudor monarchs were a. _____ and b. _____ .

2.019 The theory that a king was chosen by God and was responsible to God was called the

_____ of kings.

2.020 The Spanish Armada was a fleet of 130 _____ .

Write the letter for the correct answer on each line (each answer, 2 points).

2.021 During the Middle Ages a great deal of land in France was owned by _____ .
    a. Italy   b. England   c. Germany   d. Holland

2.022 The War of the Roses in England brought the _____ family to the throne.
    a. Tudor   b. Baskerville   c. de Medici   d. Cumberland

2.023 A movement that started in Italy and spread throughout Europe and that focused on man

in this world and a revival of Greek and Roman culture was called _____ .
    a. utilitarianism   b. hedonism   c. Lollardism   d. humanism

2.024 An Italian who wrote a manual called *The Prince*, advising rulers how to stay in power, was

_____ .
    a. Machiavelli   b. Boccaccio   c. Erasmus   d. Cervantes

2.025 A king who made himself head of a church was _____ .
    a. Louis XIII   b. Charles V   c. Henry X   d. Henry VIII

2.026 The Society of Jesus was founded by _____ .
    a. Loyola   b. Ximenez   c. John Knox   d. Copernicus

2.027 The Council of Trent in 1545 paved the way for church _____ .
    a. warfare   b. crusades   c. reform   d. moderation

2.028 Pope Paul IV drew up the first Index, a Roman Catholic list of forbidden _____ .
    a. books   b. deeds   c. cities   d. stores

2.029 Huguenots were French _____ .
    a. Presbyterians   b. Calvinists   c. Quakers   d. Anabaptists

2.030 Renaissance means _____ .
    a. absolutism   b. rebirth
    c. revival of Roman education   d. wisdom

Answer true or false (each answer, 1 point).

2.031 _____ Michelangelo is considered by many to be the greatest artist of all time.

2.032 _____ John Wycliffe was known for his attacks on the Reformation.

2.033 _____ Martin Luther was an Augustinian monk.

2.034 _____ Mercantilism was impossible under a strong central government.

2.035 _____ The Spanish Armada was a large army sent to conquer England.

2.036 _____ Guy Fawkes is best remembered for his translation of the Bible.

2.037 _____ Oliver Cromwell was a Puritan who governed England in the middle of the seventeenth century.

2.038 _____ Louis XIV was a perfect example of an absolute king.

2.039 _____ The first successful settlement by the English in the New World was at Quebec.

2.040 _____ King Henry of Portugal was called the Navigator because of his desire to explore and his interest in the sea.

66/83 SCORE_____ TEACHER_____ _____
initials date

3. REVOLUTIONS AND GLOBALIZATION

Tremendous social and intellectual change had to occur for the world to emerge from the near stagnation of the Middle Ages to the daily changes we expect in our lives today. New ideas of freedom and equality spread through the world resulting in both the American and the French revolutions and in democratic governments, such as the United States government.

The Industrial Revolution laid the groundwork for the complex technological world in which we live. It put the car in your garage, the appliances in your kitchen, and the astonishing variety of foods on your table. In this section you will look at the changes that made the modern world possible and at the modern world itself.

Section Objectives

Review these objectives. When you have completed this section, you should be able to:

16. Describe the great revolutions that helped to produce the modern world.
17. Describe the political and military career of Napoleon.
18. List the important early inventions of the Industrial Revolution.
19. Describe the events leading to and during World War I.
20. Describe the events leading to and during World War II.
21. Outline the structure of the United Nations.
22. Discuss the important political areas in the modern world.
23. List the major international organizations today.

REVOLUTIONS

Great change does not always come slowly. Sometimes it is rapid, accompanied by violence, bitterness, and hardship for many people. Even the gradual changes from the Industrial Revolution brought bloodshed and suffering as the world adjusted to new economies, social dislocation, and ways of life.

American. The road to revolution in America began with the establishment of the first English colony at Jamestown in 1607. During the sixteenth and seventeenth centuries the English contended with the Spanish and the Dutch for colonies in North America. By the eighteenth century, however, the greatest threat to the English colonies was from the French. England defeated France in the French and Indian War which ended in 1763. Then France attempted to force English colonies to pay for that war. Rebellion followed over "taxation without representation." The colonists resented supporting a government in which they had no voice. They rebelled, and the American Revolution began.

The first shots of the Revolution were fired in April, 1775, when colonists and British regular troops met and fought at Lexington and Concord in Massachusetts. In May, the Second Continental Congress met in Philadelphia. In the following year the Second Continental Congress became the first governing body in the United States. It appointed George Washington commander of the Continental army. It selected a committee of five men to write a declaration of independence. They were Thomas Jefferson, Benjamin Franklin, John Adams, Robert Livingston and Roger Sherman. On July 4, 1776 the Declaration of Independence was signed declaring the United States independent from England. The document was written by Thomas Jefferson.

In the war that followed, one-third of the colonists did not support independence from England. Furthermore, the Second Continental Congress had no power to issue taxes. It was forced to borrow the money it needed to finance the war. Soldiers were badly trained and ill equipped. At times the effort against the well trained British troops seemed hopeless.

Nevertheless, under General Washington the army rallied. In the winter of 1776, it crossed the Delaware River and defeated a thousand British and Hessian soldiers at Trenton. Thus encouraged, they went on to further victories. After an eight-year struggle, the final colonial triumph was achieved at the Battle of Yorktown. With the aid of the French who set up a blockade at sea, the colonists forced the British General Cornwallis to surrender his army in 1781. Economically drained by the war, England wanted it ended. A peace treaty was signed in Paris in 1783.

Six months before the Battle of Yorktown, the Second Continental Congress approved the first American constitution, called the Articles of Confederation. It gave Congress the authority to make war, to borrow money, to make peace, and to settle arguments between states. The Articles were ineffective, however, because they did not give Congress the power to issue taxes; and any laws passed by Congress were left to the states to enforce. These two weaknesses led to the failure of the Articles of Confederation and their replacement by the United States Constitution, which is still in effect today.

The Articles of Confederation were in effect from 1781 to 1788. Because they were weak and ineffective the new Constitution was drawn up in 1787 and adopted in 1788. In 1789 George Washington became the first President of the United States under the new Constitution.

Under the new Constitution three branches of government were created: the executive, legislative, and judicial. The Constitution created a central government strong enough to bind the states together. The Constitution's strength is its flexibility. It can be interpreted and amended to meet various needs as they arise.

The first ten amendments to the Constitution are known as the Bill of Rights. Other amendments have been added from time to time. Twenty-six amendments have been added to the United States Constitution.

Answer the following questions.

3.1 Who were the five members of the committee formed to write the Declaration of Independence?

a. _____

b. _____

c. _____

d. _____

e. _____

3.2 What was the first governing body of the United States?

_____

3.3 What did the Declaration of Independence actually do?

_____

_____

3.4 Which foreign country aided the colonists in their war against England by setting up a sea blockade? _____

3.5 What was the first United States constitution called? _____

3.6 Who was the commander of the Continental army during the Revolutionary War?

_____

3.7 What two features of the Articles of Confederation made them weak and ineffective?

a. _____

b. _____

French. Inspired by earlier revolutions in England and the United States, France experienced a revolution of its own. The French were divided into three classes: nobles, clergy, and peasants. Most work was done and most of the taxes were paid by the peasants who received little in return. They did not have the freedoms of speech, press, or worship. Trials, if they were held at all, were secret and without a jury.

Louis XVI came to the throne at the age of nineteen. He was a weak king, as his lazy and indifferent father and grandfather had been before him. France needed strong leadership. The country was bankrupt, and the oppressed people were close to revolution.

In a desperate plan to reform the government, Louis called for (1) greater freedom and encouragement of industry; (2) reduced spending of the king and his court; and (3) payment of taxes by nobles and wealthy clergy. The nobles naturally rejected the idea of being taxed on their huge incomes. Nevertheless, the government was bankrupt, and the banks would lend it no more money. The king was forced to call representatives of the people together to decide what to do.

The people's representatives quickly declared themselves a National Assembly in defiance of the absolute power of the king. They saw his desperation, and they took advantage of it. The king brought in troops to Paris where the National Assembly was meeting. Rioting followed. On July 14, 1789, the people captured the royal political prison, the Bastille, on what is still celebrated as Bastille Day in France. Riots spread to the countryside where angry and frustrated peasants killed nobles and government officials.

During the crisis the new National Assembly abolished the feudal system, which made near slaves of the common people. It adopted the Declaration of the Rights of Man. Based on ideas expressed during the American Revolution, the declaration declared freedoms

| Napoleon Bonaparte

of speech, press, and religion. It said all men were born equal and should remain equal under the law. Finally, the National Assembly adopted a constitution limiting the power of the king. When the king retaliated by plotting with the nobles to regain his full power, he was arrested; and France seemed to be without any government at all. Foreign nations, fearing the French revolutionary spirit would spread, prepared to invade France and to end the revolution themselves.

France defeated Austrian and Prussian forces and prevented the conquest of France. The New French leaders then determined to liberate all of Europe from tyranny. In the meantime, the five man Directory, which ruled the country from 1795 to 1799, proved weak and left France open to conquest. Napoleon Bonaparte rose to power, forced the Directors to resign, and dissolved the legislature. Later he crowned himself Emperor of France.

Napoleon immediately began rebuilding the military might of France. He also reorganized the government and began economic and social reforms. His government was a dictatorship, however, and his critics were dealt with severely.

Dismissing his people's desire for peace, Napoleon appealed to the new French nationalism and set out to conquer Europe. With the exception of England, all Europe fell under Napoleon's rule. His downfall began with his disastrous attempt to defeat Russia. The severe Russian winter and pursuing Russian soldiers claimed the lives of two-thirds of his six hundred thousand soldiers. Napoleon gathered another army and met the combined armies of

Austria, Russia, England, and Sweden in battle at Leipzig, Germany, in October, 1813. He was defeated there, and Paris was captured the following year. Napoleon was exiled to the island of Elba off the coast of Italy, and France was returned to its boundaries before 1792. One year later Napoleon escaped, returned to France, and raised still another huge army of enthusiastic French soldiers. Armies from all over Europe fearing the return of Napoleonic dictatorship descended on him, and Napoleon was beaten for the final time at the Battle of Waterloo in Belgium in June of 1815. This time Napoleon was banished to the island of St. Helena, located 5,000 miles from Europe, where he died at fifty-two.

 Write the letter for the correct answer on each line.

3.8 Most of the work was done, and most of the taxes were paid in pre-Revolutionary France by
_____ .

    a. big businesses   b. the middle classes
    c. peasants   d. free landowners

3.9 As kings of France, the father and grandfather of Louis XVI had been _____ .

    a. weak and indifferent   b. powerful and cruel
    c. democratic and kind   d. rich and generous

3.10 One of the reforms proposed by Louis XVI to save his country was to _____ .

    a. invade Russia   b close the Bastille
    c. tax the nobles and clergy   d. make Napoleon emperor

3.11 The Bastille in Paris was _____ .

    a. the place where the National Assembly met
    b. the king's residence
    c. a bank
    d. a prison

3.12 A document adopted by the National Assembly giving freedoms of speech, press; and religion
to all the people of France was the _____ .

    a. Declaration of Independence   b. Declaration of the Rights of Man
    c. Bill of Rights   d. Constitution

3.13 Napoleon Bonaparte eventually crowned himself _____ of France.

    a. king   b. emperor   c. president   d. protector

3.14 The decline of Napoleon and the French conquest of Europe began when Napoleon invaded
_____ .

   a. Germany   b. England   c. Italy   d. Russia

3.15 The battle in which Napoleon was beaten for the final time was fought at _____ .

   a. Waterloo   b. Leipzig   c. Elba   d. Paris

Industrial. The Industrial Revolution refers to a time when man began the wide-scale use of machines to do what had once been done by hand. Certain tasks were already being accomplished by machine. In the 1440s a German named Johann Gutenberg had invented movable type for printing books, including the famed Gutenberg *Bible*. In 1733, John Kay invented the flying shuttle, which added speed to the weaving process. James Hargreaves developed the spinning jenny in 1764, which could spin eight times as much thread as its predecessors.

In the United States Eli Whitney built the first cotton gin, which revolutionized the cotton industry and actually had such an effect on the South that it was an indirect cause of the Civil War. New methods of producing steel, rubber, and iron came into existence. The genius of Eli Whitney brought a system of interchangeable parts into existence, which led to mass production and the "car-in-every-garage" economy we have today.

New machines required new energy sources, which in turn led to the invention of more machines. James Watt in 1769 patented a steam engine that could drive other machines. In 1814 an Englishman, George Stephenson, built the first steam locomotive and the first railroad that would revolutionize transportation and travel. Robert Fulton in the United States gave the world the first steamboat, the *Clermont*.

A factory system came into existence. People no longer produced goods at home but had to work together in factories. These factories led to the explosive growth of cities which were,

| Steam tractor

unfortunately, dirty and unpleasant places to live. Factory workers lived in poverty and filth, especially in England, which was regarded as the birthplace of the Industrial Revolution.

Factories required a great deal of money to build. Money for this purpose was called *capital*, and people who invested great sums in industry were *capitalists*. Before the growth of labor unions, capitalists grew rich on the labor of workers, who were paid as little as a few cents a day to work fourteen hours in the factories. Children as young as six and seven worked as well, and no provision was ever made for their health or education. Many children in these circumstances never lived to see their twentieth birthday.

A commonly accepted date for the start of the Industrial Revolution is 1750. Before long it spread from England to the United States. New inventions included Jethro Wood's iron plow in 1819, Cyrus McCormick's reaping machine in 1834, and the threshing machine in 1836.

Industry required new transportation. Roads, such as the Cumberland Road from Cumberland Maryland, to Wheeling, Virginia, were built. The famous Erie Canal was dug to carry passengers and goods from Lake Erie to the Hudson River in New York State. In 1830 Peter Cooper built a locomotive called the *Tom Thumb*, which was the beginning of railroading in the United States.

Although they are always tragic, wars always stimulate the economies of the nations involved. The War of 1812 and the Civil War helped move the United States to the forefront as a major world economy.

Standardization of parts led to the growth of mass production in the United States. Mass production was perfected by Henry Ford in his Detroit automobile factories so that millions of cars could be produced cheaply enough to be purchased by almost everyone. Mass production has made the United States the strongest economy in the world in many ways.

As industrialization grew in the United States, the modern corporation came into being. A corporation allows many people to become stockholders in a company. This corporate structure allows more capital to be raised and companies to grow larger. Stockholders in turn grow wealthier as the companies in which they

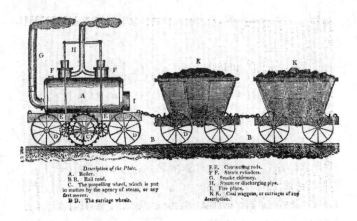

| Steam train

have invested grow more prosperous. Modern corporations are worth hundreds of billions of dollars and stretch around the world.

The Industrial Revolution had its drawbacks, many of which have been resolved. The plight of the factory workers was once desperate as they labored much like slaves in unsanitary, dangerous jobs for long hours at low wages. Labor unions arose, and after years of violence and strife, they gained the right to speak for the workers and established their right to enjoy the fruits of their labor.

Big business at one time grew into monopolies capable of crushing its opposition. This trend was curbed by such laws as the Clayton Antitrust Act of 1914, which made illegal certain methods used by big business to drive competitors out of business. Another legislative action taken to control big business was the creation of the Federal Trade Commission. Composed of five members appointed by the President, the Commission enforces antitrust laws to protect small businesses and give them a chance to survive against powerful corporations.

New Product

Invests in Product

Permission forms

Investors receive stock

Stockholders elect Company Officials

Directors

Stock Holders

President

Stockholders profit off corporate stock

| The birth of a corporation

Match these items.

3.16 _____ Fulton

3.17 _____ Gutenberg

3.18 _____ McCormick

3.19 _____ Whitney

3.20 _____ Ford

3.21 _____ Cooper

a. reaping machine

b. cotton gin

c. movable type

d. mass production

e. famed labor leader

f. first steamboat

g. built first United States locomotive

Complete the following sentences.

3.22 The birthplace of the Industrial Revolution was _____ .

3.23 A law passed in 1914 making it illegal to try to drive competitors out of business was called the _____ .

3.24 Money invested in factories and industry is called _____ .

3.25 The unfair treatment of factory workers in the early Industrial Revolution was eased by the growth of _____ .

WARS

In spite of rising prosperity, the world has fought two of the most frightful wars in history during the twentieth century. In both wars Germany was a prime aggressor, but the causes of the conflicts go deeper than that. After reviewing these two great wars you will briefly review what you have learned already about the organization established to avoid further wars.

World War I. Nationalism in Europe led to overseas expansion and colonialism by European nations. This movement was known as *imperialism*. Frictions naturally arose when nations tried to colonize the same area. Nationalism also led to the rise of strong military establishments. The German state of Prussia had adopted new military principles which became the model for the world to imitate.

By 1914 major military alliances had been formed in Europe. On one side was the *Triple Alliance*, made of Germany, Italy, and Austria-Hungary. Its purpose was to isolate Germany's enemy France from making alliances with its neighbors. Opposing the Triple Alliance was the *Triple Entente*, made up of France, England, and Russia.

The assassination on June 18, 1914, of Archduke Francis Ferdinand of Austria set off a chain reaction among European nations according to their previously arranged alliances and agreements. To avoid a long war on two fronts Germany determined to defeat France quickly and to attack Russia before the Russians were prepared to fight. Germany marched across Belgium into France, violating

Belgium's neutrality. Germany's action brought about England's decision to join with France and Russia and declare war on Germany.

Germany's attack on France at first succeeded, but it was then turned back by a courageous French counterattack. The German attack on Russia was more successful, giving the Germans confidence. The war on the Western front settled into stalemate and trench fighting by 1916 while both sides attempted to bring the United States into the war on their sides.

United States sentiment at first was against entering a European war, and President Woodrow Wilson also favored non-involvement. Germans attacked neutral shipping, however, including the *Lusitania*, in which many Americans were killed. As a result, public opinion turned, and the United States entered the war against Germany on April 6, 1917.

The entrance of the United States raised the morale of the Allies. Germany tried to end the war before the Americans could get there. It launched a massive attack on the Western front, recapturing all the land it had lost in two years of fighting. Russia had dropped out of the war after the Bolshevik Revolution of 1917, leaving Germany free to fight a one-front war in the West.

The arrival of three United States divisions stopped the German offensive at Chateau-Thierry. When the Germans began another offensive in July, the Allied forces, having been steadily reinforced with United States troops, were ready with a counterattack of their own. The Germans fell back in retreat along the Somme through the Argonne Forest. Inspired by this Allied effort, even tiny Belgium attacked the Germans.

Standing alone, Germany faced an invasion of its homeland. The German government requested an armistice. Terms were agreed upon, and an armistice was signed on November 11, 1918. World War I was the most destructive war in history up to that time.

Almost 20 million people were killed, and more than that number were wounded. Much of Europe lay in ruins.

President Wilson's Fourteen Points for a fair and lenient peace were scuttled by the vengeful allies at the Paris Peace conference. Instead, the Peace of Paris, ending World War I, contained terms that were harsh on the defeated nations, particularly Germany. It was reduced in size, occupied by foreign troops, and forced to pay huge reparations. The United States Senate rejected the treaty for political reasons, keeping the world's greatest power out of the new League of Nations. The Peace of Paris, although no one would know it, laid the groundwork for a second war twenty years later.

Answer true or false.

3.26 _____ The Triple Alliance was made up of Germany, Italy, and Austria-Hungary.

3.27 _____ The United States entered World War I because of German attacks on American colonies.

3.28 _____ The purpose of the German march into Belgium was to seize it before Russia entered the war.

3.29 _____ Most Americans, including the President of the United States, at first did not want to become involved in a European war.

3.30 _____ The *Lusitania* was sunk on orders from President Woodrow Wilson.

3.31 _____ Russia dropped out of the war against Germany after the Bolshevik Revolution of 1917.

3.32 _____ Germany requested an armistice when it faced certain invasions of its homeland.

Complete this sentence.

3.33 For political reasons the Peace of Paris and membership in the League of Nations were

rejected by the _____ .

World War II. Partly because of the war reparations, the German economy collapsed in 1923. By the 1930s Germany was solving its economic problems by rearming.

Along with military might came a desire for political power. Italy, under Benito Mussolini, invaded Ethiopia in 1935. The League of Nations, formed after World War I to prevent such attacks, did nothing. Hitler moved into the Rhineland with his troops, and no nation tried to stop him. He threatened war on Austria, and Austria gave in. He took over portions of Czechoslovakia, and his aggression was successful.

Hitler's attack on Poland in 1939, however, marked the end of the world's appeasement of the Germans. Britain and France declared war on Germany, and World War II began. By 1942 the German war machine had conquered most of Europe. Germany controlled much of North Africa, and it was about to attack its former ally, Russia.

The German invasion of Russia was its first defeat. The terrible Russian winter took its toll, and it stopped the German advance. The Russians, trained to fight in snow and cold, counterattacked and drove the Germans back.

| American troops land on Normandy Beach, D-Day, 1944

In 1941, moreover, the United States joined the war against Germany and its partners. Gradually the Allies drove the Germans from North Africa and defeated them in Italy. On June 6, 1944, a combined Allied invasion of France took place at Normandy, the largest invasion of its kind ever made. Eventually the Allies drove into Germany itself, and Berlin was surrendered to the Russians on May 2, 1945. May 8, 1945, was known as V-E Day, the day of victory for the Allied powers in Europe. The Japanese attacked the American naval base at Pearl Harbor, Hawaii, on December 7, 1941. On December 8, Congress declared war on Japan. The United States thus found itself also in a two-front war, in Europe and in the Pacific.

Fighting alone in the Pacific, the Americans decided on a policy of island-hopping. Under General Douglas MacArthur, United States forces captured islands in the Solomon, Gilbert, Marshall, and Mariana islands. Bloody battles were fought at islands with names like Tarawa, Guadalcanal, Okinawa, and Iwo Jima as the United States forces fought their way ever closer to Japan. Finally, instead of a costly invasion of the Japanese mainland, President Harry S. Truman ordered the dropping of the first atomic bomb used in war on Hiroshima, Japan, on August 6, 1945. A second bomb was dropped on Nagasaki three days later. The Japanese surrendered on August 10, 1945. World War II came to an end.

| General Assembly Hall, U.N.

United Nations. The League of Nations after World War I was established to prevent another war. The world tried again after World War II by forming the United Nations. The United Nations Charter became effective on October 24, 1945.

The main body of the United Nations is the *General Assembly*, composed of delegates from all the member nations. It acts only as a forum where views are expressed and policies are recommended. The *Security Council* is the action arm of the United Nations. It has the authority to maintain peace, to settle disputes, and to stop aggression by military means, if necessary.

The United Nations *Secretariat* is composed of clerical and administrative workers. Headed by the Secretary-General, the Secretariat contains all the permanent employees of the United Nations.

The International Court of Justice is also a part of the United Nations. It is composed of fifteen judges appointed by the Security Council and the General Assembly. It settles disputes brought to it by governments. It has no authority, however, to force nations to accept its rulings.

Complete the following sentences.

3.34 Germany's first major defeat in World War II was in _____ .

3.35 The United States was forced to fight a two-front war in World War II in

a. _____ and b. _____ .

3.36 The President of the United States who ordered the dropping of atomic bombs on Hiroshima and Nagasaki was _____ .

3.37 The beginning of World War II in Europe was brought on by Hitler's attack on _____ .

3.38 The United States declared war on Japan after the Japanese attacked the naval base at _____ .

3.39 The League of Nations showed its ineffectiveness in 1935 when it did nothing to halt Italy's invasion of _____ .

3.40 Commander of United States forces in the Pacific war was _____ _____ .

Complete the following activities.

3.41 Describe the function of the Security Council of the United Nations.

_____

_____

_____

3.42 Tell who composes the United Nations Secretariat.

_____

_____

_____

3.43 Explain who sits on the International Court of Justice and what they do.

_____

_____

_____

3.44 Give the name of the main body of the United Nations, and tell what it does.

_____

_____

_____

GLOBAL SOCIETY

Events are taking place every day in the world that affect all of us. When a revolution overthrew the government of Iran, for example, the price of gasoline at the station down the street rose visibly. In this section you will review other events that have helped shape the modern world.

Cold War. Between the end of World War II and 1991, the United States and the Soviet Union engaged in a series of confrontations that were known as the Cold War. A massive build-up of nuclear weapons by both of the post-war super powers constrained them to avoid fighting each other directly because that might have resulted in the destruction of the entire world. Instead, the Cold War was a series of limited wars (limited to a certain area with only conventional weapons) and diplomatic or ideological confrontations.

The United States led the nations of the free world in an attempt to contain communism to areas where it already existed. This effort was largely successful. The Soviet Union forcibly held Eastern Europe in the communist camp, but its successes elsewhere were few. China did become communist in 1949, but it acted independently from the Soviet Union. Despite a blockade in 1948 and the construction of the Berlin Wall around West Berlin in 1961, the section of Berlin which had been held by the western powers remained free. The Korean War (1950–1953) failed to conquer the free nation of South Korea. That war ended with a truce that divided the nation into a communist north and free south as it had been when the war began.

The communists did succeed in Vietnam and Cuba, however. The long, expensive war in Vietnam began immediately after World War II when the French fought a communist led rebel group in their southeast Asian colony. After the French withdrew, the nation was divided into a communist north and a non-communist south. The two sides fought and the United

States gradually became deeply involved in the conflict. The war became very unpopular as it dragged on and caused more American deaths. A peace treaty was signed in 1973, but it was never implemented. As the United States pulled its forces out of South Vietnam the North invaded and united the nation under a communist dictatorship in 1975.

Cuba, an island nation just 90 miles south of Florida, became communist after an internal revolution in 1959. An attempt to overthrow the government by American backed Cuban exiles in 1961 at the Bay of Pigs failed miserably. The Cuban leader, Fidel Castro, provoked one of the most dangerous confrontations of the Cold War when he attempted to install Soviet nuclear missiles in his country in 1962. The United States blockaded the island to prevent the missiles from arriving. The Soviet Union backed down about the missiles, but Cuba remained communist.

The end of the Cold War. In the mid 1980s a reform-minded leader came to power in the Soviet Union. Mikhail Gorbachev began a series of reforms aimed at improving the Soviet economy and granting a limited amount of freedom to the Soviet people. He also made it clear that the Soviet Union would no longer use its military power to support communism in eastern Europe.

The withdrawal of Soviet might doomed the communist dictatorships of Europe. One by one the nations threw out their oppressive governments and held free elections. The destruction of the Berlin Wall in 1989 is considered to be the point marking the fall of communism in Europe. It fell in the Soviet Union just two years later when an attempted coup by Gorbachev's opponents failed. In that same year, the Soviet Union was itself dissolved, creating fifteen independent republics. Thus, the Soviet Union lost the Cold War when it self-destructed.

Complete the following sentences.

3.45 A massive build up of _____ meant that the superpowers had to be concerned about destroying the world if they went to war.

3.46 Communism fell in Europe in the year a. _____ and in the Soviet Union in b. _____ .

3.47 The destruction of the _____ marked the fall of communism in Europe.

3.48 _____ began the reforms in the Soviet Union that ended the Cold War.

Complete the following activities.

3.49 Name two nations where communist aggression failed during the Cold War.

a. _____

b. _____

3.50 Name three nations that became communist during the Cold War.

a. _____

b. _____

c. _____

Changes will continue. The different regions of the world face new challenges in the post Cold War era. The countries of the world are dealing with local and internal problems as the world political structure shifts away from the Cold War battle with communism. Countries battle with terrorism and ethnic conflicts as borders are redrawn and leadership vacuums are filled.

The United States, the only remaining super power, is struggling with an economic crisis at home and battling terrorism abroad. It is trying to develop a delicate balance between its responsibilities abroad and those at home. The terrorist attacks of September 11, 2001 made the country focus on terrorist attacks against American on both foreign and domestic soil.

Eastern Europe consists of the former communist nations. These nations are all suffering the after effects of years of communist mismanagement. Bitter ethnic disputes have broken out in many of the nations. As long as the communists were in power, these disagreements were minimized. As new people and groups tried to fill the void of communism, old ethnic disagreements rose to the forefront. The former nation of Yugoslavia, in particular, has endured several years of cruel civil war between the Serbs, Croats, and Muslims who live there. Newly formed nations from the old Yugoslavia with largely ethnic boundaries have helped ease some of the tension.

The nations of Africa face repeated tribal conflicts which continuously destroy gains in the areas of industrial development, political stability, and national unity. The differing ethnic groups within the nations do not trust each other and fight each other for power. Rwanda is a good example. There, an estimated half a million people of the Tutsi tribe were killed by the rival Hutu people in 1994. Another area heavily impacted by ethnic violence is the Darfur region in the Sudan. Millions of people have been affected by ethnic violence as well as drought, famine, and displacement. The problems of one region do not remain isolated in that area. The problems of one nation spill across the border to neighboring countries. In northern Africa the situation is further complicated by groups of Islamic fundamentalists. These people use violence to try to force Islamic law upon their nations. Thus, the countries of Africa are searching for stability and unity.

The Middle East has been an area at war for most of the recent past. Wars have occurred between Jewish Israel and several of its Muslim Arab neighbors, between Iran and Iraq (1980–1988), and between Iraq and a coalition to free Kuwait (1990-1991). Iraq's dictator, Saddam Hussein, kept tensions high in the region with his promises of bringing destruction on the U.S. and its allies. Eventually the U.S. and other nations invaded Iraq with the goal of removing Hussein from power. While Saddam Hussein was successfully removed, the nation of Iraq continues to struggle with conflict among the various ethnic and religious groups. A fledgling democracy has taken hold but violence repeatedly disrupts the work of the new leaders.

In southern Asia, Afghanistan has been the site of recent wars. First Afghanistan fought against an invasion of the Soviet Union. As a result, a strict Islamic group called the Taliban took control of the country. The Taliban harbored the Al Qaeda terrorist group which was responsible for the September 11, 2001 terrorist attacks. When the Taliban refused to turn over the terrorists, the United States and its allies invaded the country. With the Taliban overthrown, the country chose democratically officials to lead. War lords continue to create problems for the new Afghanistan democracy.

Southeast Asia has moved beyond the Vietnamese War. Vietnam has invested in economic reforms and re-established relations with the west. Many of the resource rich nations of this area are becoming prosperous, but they usually have restrictive governments.

The Far East is also an area of generally growing prosperity. China began massive economic reforms after the death of Mao Zedong in 1976. It has become a booming economic powerhouse, but its people still lack some basic freedoms. Japan is both free and prosperous thanks to generous handling by the United States after its defeat in World War II. South Korea has also become prosperous since its recovery from the Korean War. North Korea, on the other hand, is desperately poor under a repressive communist government.

The legacy of the Cold War will be with the nations of the earth for many years to come. To those of us who lived to see it end, it is a privilege to see what God has done and await His plans for the future.

Answer true or false.

3.51 _____ With the exception of North Korea, the Far East is an area of growing prosperity.

3.52 _____ The Middle East has been largely peaceful in recent years.

3.53 _____ Ethnic violence is present in many countries in the world.

3.54 _____ Vietnam and China ceased to be communist in the early 1990s.

3.55 _____ The nations of Africa are divided into various ethnic groups that tend to fight each other.

3.56 _____ The nations of the former Soviet Union received a legacy of prosperity from communism.

3.57 _____ The United States is one of three superpowers remaining in the world.

3.58 _____ Iran's leader, Saddam Hussein, was eventually removed from power.

Before taking this last Self Test, you may want to do one or more of these self checks.

1. _____ Read the objectives. Determine if you can do them.
2. _____ Restudy the material related to any objectives that you cannot do.
3. _____ Use the **SQ3R** study procedure to review the material.
   a. **S**can the sections.
   b. **Q**uestion yourself again (review the questions you wrote initially).
   c. **R**ead to answer your questions.
   d. **R**ecite the answers to yourself.
   e. **R**eview areas you didn't understand.
4. _____ Review all vocabulary, activities, and Self Tests, writing a correct answer for each wrong answer.

SELF TEST 3

Answer true or false (each answer, 1 point).

3.01 _____ In the Middle Ages the Medici family ruled over the Italian city of Florence.

3.02 _____ France and Italy fought in the decisive battle of Hastings.

3.03 _____ Don Quixote was a famous Spanish poet.

3.04 _____ Henry VIII of England was known for his religious piety and good works.

3.05 _____ Bronze is made by mixing copper and tin.

3.06 _____ Genghis Khan was a Mongol invader of China.

3.07 _____ The most serious mistake Alexander the Great made was to attack Sparta.

3.08 _____ Greek civilization had its origins in the island of Crete.

3.09 _____ Greek city-states made most of their great wealth from farming and the export of agricultural products.

3.010 _____ Athens and Sparta fought one another in the Peloponnesian War.

Match these items (each answer, 2 points).

3.011 _____ Jamestown

3.012 _____ Trenton

3.013 _____ Yorktown

3.014 _____ Philadelphia

3.015 _____ Paris

3.016 _____ Leipzig

3.017 _____ Waterloo

3.018 _____ Elba

3.019 _____ Cumberland

3.020 _____ Belgium

a. island off Italy where Napoleon was sent

b. site of Second Continental Congress

c. Civil War battleground

d. first English colony

e. neutral country invaded by Germany

f. defeat of Napoleon in 1813

g. final defeat of Napoleon

h. site of National Assembly meetings

i. early American highway

j. Washington's victory over the British and Hessians

k. English surrender

Write the letter for the correct answer on each line (each answer, 2 points).

3.021 The language of the Roman Empire was _____ .
a. Latin   b. German   c. Arabic   d. French

3.022 Confucius and Buddha were both _____ .
a. Augustinian monks   b. religious thinkers
c. Italian writers   d. Roman emperors

3.023 Canute was a(n) _____ .
a. French pope   b. Scotch Presbyterian
c. Mongol warrior   d. early king of England

3.024 King Ferdinand and Queen Isabella of Spain expelled the _____ .
a. English   b. Catholics   c. Protestants   d. Moors

3.025 Leonardo da Vinci painted the _____ .
a. *Pieta*   b. Sistine Chapel   c. *Divine Comedy*   d. *Last Supper*

3.026 Holbein was a famous painter of _____ .
a. ships   b. landscapes   c. portraits   d. windmills

3.027 Martin Luther nailed his Ninety-Five Theses to a _____ .
a. monastery   b. church door   c. pole   d. wall

3.028 In 1378 the papal schism produced _____ .
a. popes   b. cathedrals   c. wars   d. doctrines

3.029 The founder of the Society of Jesus (Jesuits) was _____ .
a. Luther   b. Loyola   c. Zwingli   d. Calvin

3.030 The Spaniard who enslaved the Aztecs in Mexico was _____ .
a. Pizarro   b. da Gama   c. Inca   d. Cortez

Complete the following sentences (each answer, 3 points).

3.031 The first American constitution was called the _____ .

3.032 The first ten amendments to the United States Constitution are called the

_____ .

3.033 French society before the revolution was divided into three classes:

a. _____ , b. _____ , and c. _____ .

3.034 The man who declared himself Emperor of France was _____ .

3.035 Napoleon's downfall began with his disastrous attempt to invade _____ .

3.036 Napoleon's last battle was fought at _____ .

3.037   Gutenberg invented the movable type and printed the first books, including the _____ .

3.038   The cotton gin and a system of interchangeable parts were invented by

_____ .

3.039   In 1769 James Watt patented the first _____ .

3.040   Money invested in factories and industry is called _____ .

Answer the following questions (each answer, 3 points).

3.041   Why did Napoleon and Hitler both fail to conquer Russia?

_____

_____

3.042   What is the main body of the United Nations called? _____

3.043   What country did Hitler attack that brought France and England into the Second World War?

_____

3.044   What were the two fronts the United States fought on in World War II?

a. _____

b. _____

3.045   Why did the United States declare war on Japan in 1941?

_____

_____

83 / 104   SCORE _____   TEACHER _____ _____
initials   date

Before taking the LIFEPAC Test, you may want to do one or more of these self checks.

1. _____ Read the objectives. Check to see if you can do them.
2. _____ Restudy the material related to any objectives that you cannot do.
3. _____ Use the SQ3R study procedure to review the material.
4. _____ Review activities, Self Tests, and LIFEPAC vocabulary words.
5. _____ Restudy areas of weakness indicated by the last Self Test.

GLOSSARY

assimilation .... Absorbing into a system; making similar.

diocese .... In a church system, the territory over which a bishop presides.

hypothesize .... To assume something unproved, in order to put it to a test.

Ides of March .... The fifteenth day of March; on this day Julius Caesar was assassinated in the Roman senate.

indulgence .... The lessening of time in purgatory, according to Roman Catholic doctrine, through an act here on earth. Indulgences were sold by the Catholic clergy to such an extent during the Middle Ages that they led to scandal and corruption.

Nicene Creed .... An ancient Christian creed that begins, "I believe in one God."

scriptorium .... A copying room in a medieval monastery set aside for the copying of books and manuscripts.

see .... A cathedral town, or the territory of a bishop in a church system.

triumvirate .... A ruling body composed of three members.

vernacular .... The language of the common people in a region or country.

NOTES